What if ......

A book about friendship, coaching, dying, living, and using everything for your learning, growth and upliftment

"The pages of this book are filled with courageous authenticity and great Heart—true stories that inspire and uplift. They are tender, raw at times, and inspirational. I wholeheartedly recommend this book to anyone called to live a more purpose-driven life filled with Love and meaning. It is both poignant and filled with Spiritual Wisdom that is has been tested in the fiery crucible of lives lived all-in. True gold."

Dr. Mary R. Hulnick, Founding Faculty and Co-Director of the University of Santa Monica

"You will laugh. You will cry. You will learn. You will think. This story, authentically, poignantly, jubilantly told and ingeniously structured, is an adventure of mind and heart. It will almost certainly, as will Carolyn and Michelle, be your friend forever."

Nancy Kline, originator of the Thinking Environment; Founding Director, lead Faculty, and coach of Time to Think; and author of *The Promise that Changes Everything: I Won't Interrupt You* and *Time to Think: Listening to Ignite the Human Mind*

"This is a love story. A story of love between two friends who changed the world of coaching together. It's a funny, vulnerable, courageous book that will take you on a journey that evokes the real feelings of being human. And even though Michelle Bauman is no longer on the planet, this profound partnership lives on. Carolyn has picked up the torch of what Michelle had previously written and masterfully created a book that extends the sands of time and offers life value to anybody that reads it."

Stephen McGhee, founder of L4 Initiative (Light, Leadership, Longevity and Life), and founder of McGheeLeadership.com

"*What if This Is The Fun Part?* has the power to profoundly alter your life. In these pages you'll find a deeply touching adventure of the human spirit that takes the reader through a journey of life, death, joy, pain, and transformation. Carolyn and Michelle share how their unwavering commitment to love and service impacted everyone they met. They took what seemed to be the most difficult challenges of life and turned them into opportunities to bring joy, light, love and fun to the world. And while the book reads as a story that speaks of this beautiful relationship between friends and business partners, it is really about YOU. Carolyn and Michelle are in all of us if we allow ourselves to see it. This book, like you, is something special."

Devon Bandison, author of *Fatherhood Is Leadership*

WHAT IF THIS IS THE FUN PART?

Carolyn Freyer-Jones
& Michelle Bauman

WHAT IF THIS IS THE FUN PART?

A BOOK ABOUT FRIENDSHIP, COACHING, DYING, LIVING AND USING EVERYTHING FOR YOUR LEARNING, GROWTH AND UPLIFTMENT

What if This Is the Fun Part? A book about friendship, coaching, dying, living, and using everything for your learning, growth and upliftment.

Contact the author: carolynfreyerjones.com

Editing: Chris Nelson

Cover design: Carrie Brito

ISBN: 978-1-7379475-0-9

Library of Congress Control Number: 2021923329

First edition

This book is dedicated to Michelle. Thank you for the words, for the time, for the loving, for the beginning of our best professional lives, for saying YES to everything. I love you.

~

This book is also dedicated to friends everywhere, especially friends who believe in the life-giving, everlasting gifts of friendship that exist in and beyond the physical world.

Contents

Foreword

by Steve Chandler

This is a book about many important things and it will inspire, fascinate and enrich people in many different ways. Let me mention a few while trying to keep this foreword short enough so that I'm not preventing you from jumping right in.

It's a book about courage. You'll read the most candid and self-deprecating reflections and stories from two powerful professional women who made their whole life revolve around encouraging each other and everyone they worked and lived with. And you'll see that by "encourage" I don't mean the well-intentioned but shallow pep talks that a lot of people associate with the world of life coaching. These two, as you'll see, have mastered encouragement on a divinely deep and lasting level.

It's a book about friendship between two extraordinary women. Not just a light-hearted, "Hey, I got you, girl!" friendship full of chats, gossip and party-on encounters (though that could be there at times), but something less common. This is about friendship at the level of true love. Don't take my word for it, or mistake it for the romance-novel fictional version of the word "love," just let yourself see it as you read on. It's on every page of this book.

It's a book about loss and grief and dying way too young from cancer, but in case you are expecting to read about a gut-wrenching tragedy with a chance to pity the "victim" and a chance to curse the unfairness of life, you'll be surprised (and deeply moved) that the main characters aren't playing along with that approach.

This is a book about life coaching. But not in the narrowly professional sense (although Carolyn and Michelle have been two of the most accomplished and effective professionals in this field I have ever known), but in the larger sense of life coaching. That's the sense in which we are all life coaches in this life when we realize that to coach is to encourage. Both Carolyn and Michelle found ways to share their own courage with others and help their clients find the same courage reflected inside themselves.

This is unexpectedly also a book about humor. (Only unexpected to those readers who have no previous experience of Carolyn Freyer-Jones.) You'll be seeing the subtle humor in unexpectedly "serious" places and also uncovering the humor in everyday occurrences, and this humor is one of the "fun parts" of this book.

This is a book about the joy and power of walking your talk. I once asked my own coach, "Who coaches *you*?" He said, "My clients." I thought that was a weird answer. And I didn't really see what he meant until I had the experience of coaching Carolyn and Michelle. Then I got it. They were coaching me. Not explicitly, but by who they were being in life. Most of the time I worked with them as individuals, but I often coached them as a team when they were creating the impactful courses and seminars they delivered together. I myself grew as a coach and as a person with each encounter with these two. I wasn't really great at telling them that at the time, and now I wish I had been. When you read this book you're about to read, you'll understand what I mean. Their sheer devotion to their clients, to their families and to each other was always powerfully, sometimes even mind-bogglingly there. I didn't have to coach them on that.

Finally I want to confess that it was a very emotional experience for me to read this book. I remember visiting Michelle in the hospital near the end of her amazing life. She was so excited and happy to see me and we talked and talked until she ran out of physical energy to speak. My first thought was, "This must be a wonderful new drug they have her on . . . make note to self to find out what it is . . ." But my next thought brought me back to the reality of it: she was always this way. Drug or no drug. Circumstance or no circumstance. She would always find the joy in life and share it.

The great psychologist Nathaniel Branden once said, "You have to become what you teach." When I share that quote with coaching groups the responses I get are various nervous versions of, "Oh wow, not yet!" or "How about just becoming?" or "That's impossible, but I guess it's supposed to be the ideal."

If you think it's impossible, I will point you to Carolyn and Michelle. They have lived it.

So thanks to Scott Bauman for having recovered and agreeing to share with the world his wife's unfinished writings. And now, thanks to the marvelous writing of Carolyn Freyer-Jones, you get to read and feel for yourself what I've been trying to express right now through my tears.

Steve Chandler
Birmingham, Michigan
September 2021

Who lives? Who dies?

Who tells your story?

Hamilton

Introduction[1]

by Carolyn

I'm starting to write this introduction as I approach the sixth anniversary of the passing of my best friend and business partner. Her name is Michelle Bauman. Michelle was writing a book before she became very ill and couldn't continue. I'm going to do my best to share with you the book that Michelle was writing, adding in my own material for context along the way. Which now makes it our book.

Once upon a time we had discussed writing a book together, but the last thing we expected was that we'd do it this way.

As I read through Michelle's writing, I'm scared. Here's a sample of my thoughts:

> *Jesus, I'm scared to write this book with Michelle.*
> *She's not even alive, and I'm scared. She's a better*

---

[1] Don't skip over and jump to Chapter 1. There is critical, life-changing information in this Introduction, not to mention important details about Michelle, about conversations we had before she passed, and about the context for this book.

writer than me. She's smarter. There's so much in here. How the hell am I going to do this?

I read her writing, and I'm overwhelmed. It's almost two years since her passing, and I feel screwed. Screwed because I am concerned that people are going to read her sections of the book and think, "Damn, she was amazing. What a great woman and coach, and such a powerful writer. I'd love to have her as my coach. This Carolyn woman? Eh. She's okay. Where's the next section by this woman Michelle?"

So, lesson number one. If you read no further, BEFORE you close the book, know that you can still be jealous and run comparison with your dead business partner/best friend. You can be worried that she's going to get more clients, more accolades, more everything than you from the book—even if that's literally impossible.

Yep, that's me. An evolved, conscious, high-level professional business and life coach with a spiritual practice, and much more. Those are my thoughts.

I'm the one who's insecure and doubting and afraid that I don't have what it takes to do this. I'm judging myself as not a good enough writer, person, coach, friend—you name it.

That's me at a low place. If you read this entire book, you'll learn that I, like anyone, can get low. I see the part of me that judges myself, and I can also see the part of me that thinks it's funny to write about being jealous of a dead best friend.

And then there's the part of me—the deeper, wiser part—that

can practice Compassionate Self-Forgiveness (a tool taught at the University of Santa Monica in their Spiritual Psychology program).

I forgive myself for judging myself as less than.

I forgive myself for forgetting that there's no such thing as better than or less than.

I forgive myself for buying into the misinterpretation of reality that loving can be measured or "won."

I forgive myself for judging myself as a crappy writer and person.

I forgive myself for judging myself as a lousy best friend for being (temporarily) competitive with my dead business partner.

I forgive myself for forgetting that I am not my thoughts.

I forgive myself for forgetting that I can choose which thoughts I listen to.

FYI, Michelle would laugh a lot about me being concerned with how people would receive her and me in this book. Her response would be, "You're amazing!! This is ridiculous. And remember: you always ended up making more money than me, so who's jealous of whom??"

It's important to know that I came to my friendship with Michelle as a solid, successful person with enormous amounts of personal growth work under my belt. We were professional equals—each very different, and very similar.

All the same, there's no replacing Michelle. To those of you who read this and think, "Why couldn't the other one have died? Michelle was awesome . . . I would have loved to have worked with her"—I understand. There are people in our community who wish

Michelle was still here, who prefer her over me. I get it. I don't take this personally; it's understandable. She was amazing, and different than me.

My response to those who wish Michelle was still here is, "Yep, me too. I'm who's left, though."

What if this is the Fun Part—Using Everything for your Learning, Growth, and Upliftment

First and foremost this book is a love story. A love story between two friends. I expressed this to Michelle's husband, Scott, not long ago, when and he was asking about the book. I updated him on where it was, and that's the phrase that came out: "Well, Scott, in most ways the book is a love story of two friends."

He laughed and said, "I remember sometimes Michelle would say to me after texting with you, 'Carolyn is going to XYZ with so and so, and she had this thing happen'—and she'd tell me what you were doing. And I remember thinking, 'And I care about this because?'"

Exactly. That's how connected Michelle and I were in each other's minds; that's where we were at in our friendship. She would relate my day to her husband almost as if it were as relevant to him as her own.

AND, this book is also a love story about professional coaching—the transformative coaching we received from our beloved coach, Steve Chandler, the coaching we did together, the coaching Michelle did on her own, and the coaching I do now.

It's also a love story of learning and living—for the long haul—the principles and practices of Spiritual Psychology as taught at the

University of Santa Monica.

And it's also a love story of living, loving and dying fully. A love story about learning how to use everything for your learning, growth and upliftment.

Michelle developed the title *What if This Is the Fun Part?* through her coaching with Steve Chandler, her life, and her work coaching others. You'll see that one of her chapters talks about this.

I added "a book about living, loving, dying, coaching, improving your work and your life, and using everything for your learning, growth, and upliftment."[2]

Yes, that's what you read. Everything. Including dying, or watching someone you love die. That's not what I had wanted or planned to be doing, but this is what happened. Cooperating with what *is* is one of the most difficult life lessons, but it's one that will result in great maturing, both spiritually and in general.

During Michelle's final two to three weeks in the hospital we had a few very important, pivotal conversations. A key one came shortly after she had been intubated and was unconscious. When the intubation occurred, it began to dawn on me that Michelle might not ever speak with me again—a shocking, devastating thought. Michelle was one of the most beautiful and funny communicators I knew.

Then, not surprisingly knowing her, Michelle had a short rally where she communicated again.

She couldn't actually speak at that point. She was on a ventilator, so she communicated by "talking" around the ventilator. She wrote

---

[2] And then I trimmed it so it would fit on the front cover.

very messy letters and words on a notepad (her fingers were puffy from the medications and her illness), and she used cards they give you in the ICU printed with letters and pictures and words you can point at. (Given where we are today, I would have thought someone might have invented a more effective technological solution using an iPad or something like that, but there wasn't anything like this in the ICU.)

I was with her in the hospital, slowly explaining that her husband Scott and I had thought she might die when she was intubated, that she might not come back. I shared with her that Scott had asked me if I thought Ron and Mary (Drs. Ron and Mary Hulnick, the co-directors of the University of Santa Monica and our teachers, mentors, and the developers of the principles and practices of Spiritual Psychology) would be willing to have her service at USM.

She looked at me and mouthed/spoke/wrote, "And you'd be the MC of my service, right?"

I looked at her and slowly answered, "If that's what you want."

She then mouthed/spoke/wrote, "If I die, I don't ever want it said that I died after a 'long, hard battle' with cancer. It has not been a battle. I have had joy every day."

I looked at her again and said, "I hear you. No long, hard battle with cancer, got it. And—joy every day. Really, though? I mean, joy even in *this*?" I glanced around the room, and pointed at the cards and paper where we were trying to figure out what she was trying to communicate.

"Yes, even this. This is fun," she said, smiling, looking at the cards.

"Okay, I hear you," I said. I was stunned, but I knew what she was saying was important.

But even here you can see this book's title and message in play. What if *this* is the fun part? "This" meaning *everything*. What if you can use everything for your learning, growth, and upliftment? Including lying in a hospital bed with cancer, struggling to communicate with your best friend? Or *being* that best friend and watching your best friend (or your wife, husband, child, mother, father) dying?

Or war.

Or famine, illness, the homeless, child abuse, our government, aging . . .

There are no sacred cows in using everything for your learning, growth, and upliftment.

This is not a small thing to accept or choose as a context for life. And you may decide right now that you do NOT want to learn more about this. You may be angry that I even wrote that this is a possible context and approach to life.

I understand. I don't live it 24/7. My intention is to keep growing into this. The alternative—what I was living before, no real context other than victimhood and fear—was pretty miserable and unsatisfying.

This is what Michelle was writing about before she died. This is what she was living into right to the end.

And now, on her behalf, I'd like to invite you to join us in exploring what it's like to live as if it were true.

~

This book is written in chapters, some by Michelle and some by me. I make it clear when it's Michelle's piece, and I also try to place it in the context of where she was at in her life when she wrote it.

Some of her pieces are not finished. I included them anyway because I felt they were so impactful. Occasionally I will add my own commentary after her pieces, if it seems like it could be useful. At the end of the book I've also included Michelle's 2014 talk at Claremont College, her alma matter, which beautifully captures so much of what she was about. Finally, the closing pages of the book contain remembrances of her by seven women whose lives she touched.

Now, let's back up further, to the beginning, and allow Michelle to set everything up.

— 1

How We Became CarolynandMichelle

by Michelle

Once upon a time there were two friends who loved each other very much. At first the two friends worked out at the same gym so they saw each other almost every morning. Then things changed and they both stopped going to the gym, so they had to find other ways to stay connected. Given their full lives of family, work and kids, this wasn't always easy. No matter how much time they squeezed in to talk, it never seemed like enough.

One day they were talking on the phone, each sitting in an office at their respective corporate jobs (which they had held for over a decade). One said wistfully to the other, "Wouldn't it be fun if we worked together?"

"That would be AWESOME!" the other replied.

Neither of them knew it at the time, but that wish was actually a prayer—a prayer that was answered.

It would be a few years before that seed of a prayer began to sprout. But what was planted with love eventually bore the fruit of that love.

There Is no USM for Michelle Without Carolyn

Without Carolyn, I would never have found my way to the University of Santa Monica (USM). USM is a special place that does one thing, and one thing only: it promotes the principles and practices of Spiritual Psychology world-wide. Its programs are designed to support students in answering three questions:

1. Who am I?
2. What is my purpose?
3. How can I make a meaningful difference?

The work of answering these questions is deep and transformational. My USM education literally changed my life and the life of my family.[3]

When I first met Carolyn at the gym, I had no spiritual practice, no interest in transformation, and certainly no intention of enrolling in a two-year master's degree program. Sure, I was feeling unhappy, stuck and frustrated—but that information was not for public knowledge. Besides, I was pretty sure that if I could just lose that last seven or eight pounds, my life would be perfect.

Not only was Carolyn a USM graduate (she got her degree in 1998), she also served as the University's Director of Admissions— a position that she held for more than twelve years. When Carolyn first told me what she did for a living, I deemed her "weird" and proceeded not to talk to her for a month. (Back away from the crazy lady. Do not make eye contact. Do not engage.)

But Carolyn is so darn grounded, fun, compassionate and interesting that it was hard for me to stay away from her. And, in my own defense, we were working out at a very intense gym at five-

---

[3] For more information about USM, check out their website, especially the videos: www.universityofsantamonica.edu

thirty in the morning, three days a week. That in and of itself was a bit crazy. So who was I to judge?

One day I arrived at the gym in the midst of a professional crisis. I had just transferred from one division to another at my job, thinking that this change would be the answer to my frustration and lack of fulfillment. But after only a week at the new job, I had a pretty strong sense that I had made a huge mistake and that this new position was going to be even less fulfilling than the one I had left.

Usually, I do a pretty good job of covering up how I feel (especially back in 2006). I tend to run the script called "everything is great." But that particular day at the gym, my level of fear and panic was so active that I couldn't hold it back. When Carolyn sat down on the recumbent bike next to mine and lightly asked, "How are you?" I burst into tears.

I complained to her that I basically had to come to terms with the fact that my life was going to be the way it was. All the big decisions had been made; I was stuck with this job, making this amount of money, this husband, these kids, this house, and so on. I simply needed to resign myself to the fact that my life wasn't likely to change much.

Her response shocked me. She said, "You don't know that that's true."

With that one sentence she challenged my whole assumption. In fact, before she spoke, I didn't even know I was making an assumption; I thought I was simply seeing the truth.

In that moment, I was coached for the very first time. And, by such a gifted and compassionate coach!

I Got More Interested in What's Possible

After that first conversation, Carolyn and I talked more about her USM education and her own transformation. She gave me a few really powerful books: *The Four Agreements* by Don Ruiz Miguel, *Leadership and Self-Deception* by the Arbinger Group, and *Ten Commitments to Your Success* by some guy called Steve Chandler (more on him later).

Just in reading these books, my life started to change.

Without realizing it, I had begun to feel as though my life didn't have much meaning. But when I cracked open those books, I started to see that it was up to me to *make* meaning. Steve's book in particular challenged me to make the difference that's available to me in the moment, the difference I can make right *now*, and not to wait for some time in the future when I have all my ducks in a row. So I started looking around me in the moment to see how to make that difference: pick up a piece of trash, return my shopping cart to the rack at Trader Joe's, help my husband pick out a tie . . . In doing this I had such a different experience in my own life. I saw that I mattered.

I still had no intention of going to USM right then. I told Carolyn, "I'll go when my kids are in college and I'm ready to transition to something else." My kids were seven and five at the time.

Carolyn has since told me that when I told her this, she thought, "Wow, that's an awfully long time to wait."

To her credit, she didn't say anything then.

Needless to say, I soon had a change of heart. (That's another story—too long to put here, but I promise I'll write about it soon; it's a great story.) The call to attend USM that very year grew stronger and stronger . . . and I'm so, so grateful I answered it!

Things Really Started to Change for Me at USM

Anyone who spends time with me knows how much I love the University of Santa Monica. I basically haven't left since the day I walked through the doors as a workshop participant in June of

2006. I've returned every year as either a student or a volunteer.

Why do I keep coming back? Because my life gets better and better the more time I spend there.

What I mean by this is that there is more peace and love inside of me and in my home the more I focus on my personal growth. Plus, I find that the more I do my own work, the more effective I am facilitating the work of others.

But here's the bottom line: not everyone is going to USM. Being a USM student requires a high level of commitment. Class is held one weekend a month—and it's a REALLY long weekend. The hours alone are enough to keep my husband from ever considering attending.[4]

During my second year at USM, I became acutely aware of how much my life was changing. For example, I was used to being someone who worried all the time. I worried about having enough money, about someone getting sick, and so on. All the usual stuff and more. In fact, I ruined two days of my honeymoon in beautiful Bali because I was worried that I left the toaster on, that my mother was angry at me and that I had misplaced my mother-in-law's garter. TWO DAYS!

Before USM, I would wake up in the middle of the night several times a week, wracked with anxiety. I'd feel pressure in my chest, tightness in my jaw, shortness of breath. My mind would be churning with a sense of panic I could do nothing about. For decades, I had no idea how to work with this, so I would just get out of bed and read or play Minesweeper on the computer. In fact, I didn't think there was anything *to* do; I just thought, "This is the way I am."

It never occurred to me that I could work with that anxiety or

[4] Note from Carolyn: Michelle's husband, Scott, attended USM the year following her passing. The hours didn't get in his way.

change my thinking. And while it was bad enough to be annoying, it wasn't so debilitating that I actually sought help.

The tools and skills I was learning at USM were so effective that this pattern of anxiety disappeared. I started easily sleeping through the night. My insomnia never really returned—only on very rare occasions do I wake up in the middle of the night feeling anxious, and now I know how to work with these feelings in a loving and effective way.

Another thing: before USM I had a lifelong fear of failure. My whole game in life was to preserve the illusion that I am smart, "better than" and nice. Almost every decision I made in my life between the ages of thirteen and thirty-nine was made at least in part to bolster that image of myself, including the person I married and my decision to become a lawyer.

As my USM education progressed, I discovered within myself a greater willingness to take risks and FAIL. I was used to walking around with my stomach clenched, waiting for the force of a mistake or failure to sock me in the gut. Now, somehow, things were starting to loosen up.

Not Everyone Is Going to Attend USM

As I moved on from my USM education, I felt happier, freer, younger and more hopeful than I had ever felt. And as I looked around my world, I saw so many talented, capable people—particularly women—who were in exactly the same place I had been before starting my journey. They didn't understand how to take dominion over their thoughts. They were racked with worries and saddled with the belief that they were responsible for everyone else's feelings; consequently, they also experienced the resentment that comes from always putting yourself last.

That's how I used to be!

I talked about my experiences with my friends and the other women I knew. Although I detected a twinkle of hope and possibility in their eyes—that sense that things *could* be different—I didn't see any of them rushing the admissions office at USM. This may have been disappointing, but it wasn't surprising. After all, it's a financial and time commitment to attend USM, and classes only start in October. For these reasons and others, USM is not a fit for everyone.

Thinking about this, I realized that there was a real need for learning new ways to live life. But could I teach them? Could I create an environment where I could serve people, where growth would occur?

I had no idea, but with my newfound willingness to take chances, I decided to try. As part of my graduate school program, I created a four-hour workshop called "Simple Shifts: Straightforward Strategies for Positive Change." I thought of twenty or so friends whom I thought might be interested, and I drafted an email inviting them to participate.

Hitting send on that email was one of the most terrifying experiences of my life. In many ways, it was my "coming out" as a coach. Many of the women didn't know I was attending USM and that I had started coaching. I had no idea what they thought of coaching—let alone of ME as a coach.

The thought of hitting send made me feel like I was opening myself up to public ridicule, shame, embarrassment.

But I did it anyway.

The feedback was immediate and positive. Within forty-five minutes the workshop was full, and I decided to add a second workshop to handle the overflow.

Carolyn:

I love Michelle's sharing of this story. This is where CarolynandMichelle were born. And it was good.

Now you might be thinking, "Okay, I get it. So this Michelle person really liked USM. But what does she mean by "A high level of commitment?" What exactly did USM require her to commit to? What went on there that was so life-changing for her? And what happened in her friendship with me?

All good questions. Let's take them one at a time.

USM is a place where one digs deep into one's life, in real time. You learn to apply the principles and practices of Spiritual Psychology, and related tools and skills, to your life—past, present and future. This is very different from a traditional education. In the USM classroom, everything happening in your life goes into the room with you. This means the things you "know" about yourself as well as the things lurking inside of you that are hidden from your everyday awareness. Those unresolved issues that lie sleeping— except for when they leak to the surface in your work, your marriage, and so on.

That said, there's no requirement to go on archeological digs at USM. Nothing is forced. The curriculum is designed to surface what hasn't been handled, but as Dr. Mary Hulnick, co-Director and primary faculty member of USM, says to students: "What's meant to surface for you to work with will surface."

For Michelle, this meant her childhood, where she learned how to be a "good girl" who was devoted to external achievement and validation. This also meant her early days as a mother, where she screamed a lot and was angry that she was tired, angry at her husband that she was tired, and angry at the world that she was tired.

In the present, it meant her work as a lawyer, where she was feeling dissatisfied and wanting more fulfillment. She was also experiencing a deep yearning for a spiritual connection that she didn't even realize she yearned for until she was sitting in the classroom at USM and was shown the possibility that perhaps there was a spiritual context for life.

Michelle risked a lot walking into the USM classroom. Her husband Scott was skeptical and nervous. He had concerns that the program might somehow affect her and pull her away from him and their boys. Michelle had this fear as well.

So we had an honest conversation about it. As the Admissions Director at USM, I had listened to many, many people express their concerns about what going through the USM program might do to their marriage. My response was always more or less the same: "Your marriage might get stronger; that happens for people. For others, it exposes cracks that were already there. Those cracks might get filled in with feelings of greater peace and connection. Or for some, the exposed cracks might lead to a completion in the marriage, one that was being avoided. If that happened, wouldn't it be better to deal with it sooner rather than later?"

In Michelle's case, her USM education brought greater peace and acceptance into her marriage. She became less judgmental with Scott and more willing to ask for what she wanted. She became a more awake and connected mother, one who yelled less and worked with her own material so that she wasn't taking it out on her boys. Spiritually, Michelle had a significant awakening to her own Divine nature, something we talked about a lot.

Because I had already graduated from USM, all of these

conversations with Michelle about what was happening for her were tremendously exciting for me. I was walking through the program again, only now it was through her eyes. Everything was fresh and new, and she and I became closer with each class weekend she participated in.

Finally, Michelle's comment that "USM is not for everyone" refers to several aspects of the program. First, there is the amount of time the program requires: eighteen full-class weekends, beginning Friday night and running through Sunday evening, over the course of two years, plus a weeklong class each summer. Add to this the significant homework and reading assignments. Finally, tack on the discomfort of ALL of one's limiting beliefs and painful narratives coming to the surface for healing and the final tally = not for everyone. The program is extraordinary, but it's not for the faint of heart.

It was, however, for Michelle, and through it she began to step into the possibility of her life becoming truly different—from the inside out.

— 2 ———————————————

Near Death

by Michelle

I'm intrigued by near-death experiences. According to the Near Death Experience Research Foundation (or NDERF), millions of people of all ages and from all walks of life have reported near-death experiences. In fact the NDERF estimates that 774 Americans *per day* have near-death experiences. This includes people who don't believe in an afterlife or have a spiritual orientation.

Those who have come very close to death tell strikingly similar stories: they leave their body and observe the room (or other setting) that they're in from above. At first they feel scared, and then calm, and then they see an incredible light and experience a deep and wonderful sense of knowing and peace.

I had a different kind of near-death experience. There was no dramatic, life-threatening incident, no hospital or physical crisis. But still, I almost died, and what's more, I almost missed it. In fact, I had no idea how close to death I was. I thought I was living. I had done everything right. I was working as a lawyer, married to a wonderful man, and had two kids and a mortgage. I fully bought into the idea that conventional choices were my path to fulfillment, but instead of finding nirvana at the end of the rainbow, it was more like the movie *Groundhog Day*—an endless loop of activity without feeling like I was getting anywhere.

What trapped me in near-death was a belief that at age forty my life was basically going to be what it already was; the big choices had been made. Excitement and possibility were experiences of my past. My only option was to suck it up and live out my choices.

It wasn't the job, husband or kids that were the problem. In fact, there was nothing wrong with any of the choices I had made. Rather, it was a belief that I was done growing; this was what dulled my sense of aliveness and left me angry, without a clear cause.

It is only in looking back that I can appreciate what a close call that was. How easily I could have continued to feel resentful and trapped by the choices I had made! How socially acceptable it was! How little experience or guidance I had for listening to the part of me that was screaming: ARE YOU KIDDING ME? THIS CAN'T BE ALL THERE IS!

Reconnecting with myself as a powerful creator, someone who is actively engaged in learning, growing and evolving, has breathed joy and adventure into my life that I didn't know was missing. Before, I was a facsimile of myself, kind of like those two-dimensional cutouts of celebrities you see in the movie theater lobby. But now I'm much more fleshed-out and full.

And as it turns out, surviving this type of near-death experience is not a one-time event. Now I battle mini near-deaths, sometimes daily. The hum of the everyday is a powerful lullaby. If I'm not paying attention, my eyelids start to get heavy and the comfort of going through the motions is as seductive as an old pair of sweatpants.

I wonder what I have in common with people who have had traditional near-death experiences. Do they work hard to keep the wonder of their NDE alive inside of them to inform their present? Do they struggle to find the language to help others understand their unique experience? Do they dance with the curious wonderings of what more lies ahead, thinking, *What else will I experience as I choose the pulse of aliveness?*

Carolyn:

One of the jobs I have in co-writing this book is choosing. Choosing from Michelle's writing, deciding where it goes, if it makes sense, and if it "fits" with the book.

This piece is really important to give you a taste of who Michelle was and is.

I had not read any of this work until Michelle's husband, Scott, handed me the electronic files in October of 2017. I was aware that she had been writing it, and had seen some of the pieces Michelle and I used in our work together. But I hadn't seen the bulk of it.

When Michelle woke up from her Groundhog Day it was an explosion. Some people wake up more slowly. They hang onto their old paradigms until they gradually realize that hitting their head against the same wall over and over isn't getting them anywhere. Michelle's lightning intelligence and huge heart somehow put her on a fast track; it was like she was awakening on speed. The false assumptions she'd been living as true fell away rapidly. She didn't hang onto them the way some people do.

Like me, for example. I was pretty attached to being a victim and holding my parents accountable for all of the wrongs in my life. It took me well into my second year of USM to start shaking these beliefs. I had done my initial "wake up" in 1996, and I thought I was pretty deep into my own process when Michelle and I met in 2002. I had already graduated from USM and was working there. I was also being coached by Steve Chandler and doing a little of my own coaching on the side.

Michelle was so smart, and she was forty when her awakening occurred, so she was in a very different phase of her life than I had been at twenty-nine.

I love this:

The hum of the everyday is a powerful lullaby. If I'm not paying attention, my eyelids start to get heavy and the comfort of going through the motions is as seductive as an old pair of sweatpants.

3

Our Work

by Carolyn

December 14th.

Today is the anniversary of Michelle's last day on Earth.

"I miss her" is an understatement.

Those words don't even begin to capture the feeling.

"I miss Michelle" is so vast, so huge . . . Those words aren't enough to touch the bigness of how much I miss Michelle's presence here.

Michelle is the reason I am more generous now.

Michelle is the reason I am a more loving wife now.

Michelle is the reason I am a less judgmental person now.

Michelle is the reason I am a full-time professional coach now.

Michelle is the reason I am a *better* coach now.

Michelle is the reason I am more willing to connect now.

Michelle is the reason I am a writer now.

When Michelle and I started working together, we coached groups of women and focused on creating greater fulfillment and joy in life. Michelle came up with the name "InnerWow."

Shortly thereafter I hated that name . . . and we kept it for a pretty long time. Why? Because in some areas, we were, let's say . . . lazy. Or, to be more generous, uninterested in handling more "administrative" things.

Our coach, Steve Chandler—a master coach and teacher of coaches—would often say to us, "You don't need to do anything other than connect and talk to people." Connecting with and serving other people would allow us to grow a thriving, professional coaching business.

So for a long time, neither of us had a web site (and we each made our first $100k without one). We didn't do anything on social media. We didn't write anything. Branding? Blech—and my background was marketing!

We had children, we had husbands, we had work. We had full lives and really didn't like doing anything "extra" (I still don't). But we each had six-figure coaching practices within the first year of going full time.[5]

What Michelle and I *did* like was serving people, coaching, connecting, and creating communities and groups where

---

[5] Sidenote for coaches or any service industry: This is not in any way to say that websites are not of value, or that one shouldn't use social media, or write, or do videos. If you love these, wonderful. They can be great things to do to share who you are and provide value. But as Steve taught us, it's just not *necessary*. If you never want to do those things you can still grow a thriving business, one deep conversation at a time. Eventually you'll want a website, because now it's required so that people can see that you're "real." But a website alone won't get anyone a client. It might lead to someone contacting you, but from there . . . yes, you will need to know how to talk to people and help them.

transformation could occur.

InnerWow was about the inner experience that occurred in people doing the work we facilitated. I hated the name pretty quickly because it felt like some kind of sparkly drink. It was bubbly and fluffy. I'm not fluffy, and neither was Michelle.

We were, however, sparkly—Michelle and I both—in a particular way. Not superficially sparkly. Michelle was a sparkly that ran deep. She was like one of those rocks that sparkles on the outside, so you pick it up. Then when you break it open you discover that it sparkles all the way through in a mesmerizing way.

The name InnerWow didn't feel deep enough, intelligent enough, rich enough for what we did, at least not to me. And we would laugh about it. I would share how much it didn't capture us fully, but we kept right on using it, because changing it would require changing handouts and other things that neither of us liked to do. That kind of work was not, in our view, "fun." (Even though it could have been, with the proper mindset. We were aware of that—we were coaches!)

So we kept it for about two years, and Michelle's email address always had "InnerWow" in it. We eventually morphed the name for the group work we did with women into what I use now: "Self-Mastery for Women."

Initially our InnerWow groups were held in the family room of Michelle's house. We offered half-day, complimentary events first, inviting as many women as we could fit to go through an afternoon of real work. Here they could hit "pause" on their lives, slow down, go inside, and see what was missing, what wasn't working, or what was calling them.

Michelle and I started the day by introducing each other—or

rather, by "creating" each other, because as our coach Steve pointed out, this was much more effective. Michelle could create me with words that wouldn't work if I were to say them about myself. And I could create Michelle in ways she couldn't, because from her it would appear self-serving and ego-centered.

By "create" I mean *bring to life in a very specific way*. Creating in this sense is more than simply introducing. To create someone is to share about them in a way that highlights who they are so generously that the audience gasps and has an inner experience of, "What would it be like to have someone talk about me this way?"

Here's an example of how Michelle would create me:

"Many of you know Carolyn and I well. And for many of you this is your first experience of us. So I am going to take a minute to introduce you to Carolyn Freyer-Jones. We literally would not be here doing this work today if it weren't for Carolyn. I met her at the gym in June of 2004. At the time I fancied myself fairly successful and happy, but it was clear to me that Carolyn had a whole different skillset than me. She is such a pillar of strength, of compassion, wisdom, flexibility, resilience. She is so joyful and full of hope and possibility. When I first met her I was intrigued, and her example started me on the path that led me to this work. Carolyn graduated from the University of Santa Monica in 1998 with a Master's Degree in Spiritual Psychology. After that she worked at USM for twelve years, much of that time as the Director of Admissions and Marketing, coaching and working with thousands of potential applicants. She has been a full-time coach for over nine years. She has a three-and-a-half-year-old daughter and a great husband. The way she does her life—with a high level of impeccability, joy and commitment—continues to inspire me. My life has been transformed because of her.

It is such privilege to be with her when she is coaching people. She has an incredible ability to create a context for the challenges or opportunities her clients face. She is willing to tell them the truth with so much love and compassion that they can really hear it— maybe for the first time. And she is a master in supporting them in discovering their own strength and courage. I'm thrilled for each of you to have the chance to work with her today, and I encourage you to take full advantage of this opportunity."

I share this with you because it provides you with context for the ways in which Michelle and I served each other and loved each other. To be introduced by Michelle in this way was something I had never experienced before in my life. Cherishing and loving and appreciating so wholeheartedly was something Michelle did with ease, it was so "right" for us to do this with each other (I have a great husband—he just doesn't talk this way about me). And, since we did it often, I absolutely began to take it for granted. Not that I didn't appreciate it; I simply thought it would always be there.

We started to offer our four-month "Co-creating Your Inspired Life" coaching group. We learned a lot along the way.

We enrolled ten women into each group through heartfelt conversations. We listened, we acknowledged, and we shared a vision for what was possible in the group. And we learned how to enroll without attachment. Or, or at the very least, when we became attached to the outcome we had our coach assist us in seeing how this didn't serve—how it actually made people go away, because nobody likes a desperate, attached coach. That's like client-repellant.

The Best Days

The early days of growing our businesses, both together and individually, were some of the best days of my life. Coaching people over the phone as I sat on the floor of my bathroom in the one-bedroom apartment I shared with my husband, or sitting in my car in the carport . . . I remember standing in Michelle's messy kitchen as we planned our next meeting with our group, reviewing the spectacular errors we'd made in our earlier efforts. All the while we were being coached into serving in stronger ways. It was all great, even—or especially—the messy parts: the e-mail we sent out with an error in it, the group participant who disappeared and then revealed she was "upset" with us for calling her forward into greater participation . . . It was all amazing.

I consider myself one of the most privileged people to have experienced such joy in the creative, challenging, grueling, fun, magical process of building a business. I attribute this experience largely to the quality of relationship Michelle and I had. Without Michelle I can easily see how it could have been a real @#!% show, with drama, chaos and many unsuccessful attempts to create something that ended in misery and disappointment. High-functioning, close, mutually respectful and successful business partnerships and friendships are not common—even with the most evolved people. (I'm not suggesting that Michelle and I were "most evolved" people, only pointing out that even when all your ducks are in a row, things can go horribly south.)

We were very well-suited for each other. We shared a willingness to get messy, to be imperfect, to be bold in the world and our community, to not apologize for charging strong fees and to carve out our own place in the world of transformation—one group of women at a time.

How Does One Continue?

I am still in this question. How does one continue "after" a friendship and partnership like this? I don't know. Yet I am continuing. I am committed to continuing, to continuing my vibrant life, my vibrant work, my vibrant intention to learn and grow and use everything for my learning and growth.

I am receiving a powerful kind of coaching from Michelle, or rather from life in general as channeled through my relationship with her. And it's all about being right here, right now.

Because I still have moments and days where I long for Michelle to be here, now, in the physical. Longing, longing, longing. Longing leads to suffering, though, so I work to not hang out in the longing. WHY? You might ask, "What's wrong with longing?"

Longing puts me (and you) smack in the middle of "not now," of wishing something were occurring that clearly cannot currently occur. It takes us WAY out of the present.

I miss Michelle more than I can write about. I am almost breathless sometimes, when the missing punches me in the gut. At the same time I am committed to what's right NOW. Right in front of me there are people who are calling me, asking me questions, wanting my attention and presence. There's my husband, my daughter, dear friends and clients whom I serve. They all want my full awareness, and that's something I know can only happen if I turn away from the longing and towards them.

I choose to remember that Michelle's bright and shining love is right here, in my heart, where I can access her. I remember that

Michelle's loving opened doors for me that will never close, as long as I continue.

— 4

How to Relate to "Super Stars"

by Michelle

Sometimes I wish Carolyn wasn't so great at what she does. I wish she wasn't such a strong and powerful coach. I wish she wasn't so fearless and bold. I wish she would pull back. Dim her light. Take a break. I wish she wasn't always "going for the learnings." I wish she was more insecure about whether her fees are "worth it." I wish she worried more about where her next client was coming from. Basically I wish she'd play a smaller game.

Every time she raises her fees, I groan. Every time she suggests we do something new in our business, I resist. When she starts to get that sparkle in her eye, that jump in her step that signals some new possibility . . . I want to hide.

These wishes operate at a barely conscious level. It's a little embarrassing for me to share them. What kind of supportive partner and friend am I to wish my friend would be less than who she is?

In fact, these thoughts get buried under irritation and annoyance. They are disguised as judgments. In fact, if I didn't love her so much and have so much respect for who she is as a friend and a woman, as well as a coach, I would most likely pick her apart, make her wrong.

Why do I do this? Because there is some part of me that wants everyone I know to make an agreement that we will ALL be less than we are. I want everyone to agree to be less—so I can get away with being less.

How do I know this is operating? Because when I see someone shining brightly, one of my first instincts can be to find fault, to see where that bright shiner doesn't measure up, to criticize her parenting, or her looks, or her weight, to put her in some different category than me—so I can still pretend that I am doing my best, pretend I'm not scared to shine, that I'm not scared to get "big" and have people judge me or not like me.

When I take responsibility for the irritation that's happening within me, when I can see the judgments that I generate from inside myself, I find fear lurking in the shadows inside me, fear that sends up smoke screens of judgment and irritation in an attempt to remain hidden. After all, if I can negatively judge people whom I perceive to be more courageous (or more successful or more talented) than me, then I'm off the hook.

But the real truth came out of my own mouth a few years ago when Carolyn and I were at lunch with a fabulous business coach we both know. He was asking us questions about our business and our fees. At the time, Carolyn's fee for individual coaching was higher than mine. He looked at me and asked, "Why are her fees higher?" and I blurted out the most truthful answer without even thinking: "Because she is more courageous than I am."

Carolyn:

Can you imagine my surprise when I read this piece? It was the first piece I opened after Michelle's husband Scott gave me the files. It wasn't finished—there were a few more sentences that started to build upon what you see above, but I've left them out because this first part of the piece is complete in itself.

I chose to include this piece, because, well, it's fantastic. Not because it's in part about me, but because it has a lot of important messages in it, for both women and men.

THIS:

Why do I do this? Because there is some part of me that wants everyone to make an agreement that we will ALL be less than we are. I want everyone to agree to be less—so I can get away with being less.

How do I know this is operating? Because when I see someone shining brightly—one of my first instincts can be to find fault, to see where that bright shiner doesn't measure up, to criticize her parenting, or her looks, or her weight, to put her in some different category than me—so I can still pretend that I am doing my best, pretend I'm not scared to shine, that I'm not scared to get "big" and have people judge me or not like me.

This is so powerful. I saw myself in it right away.

That's right: I do exactly what Michelle was doing about me. In fact, I did this about Michelle. She always wanted to evolve the handouts we used, make everything "better" every time we did it, with this question in mind: "Is this the most transformative way we can serve these women?"

This always triggered me, as in, "WHY DO WE HAVE TO WORK SO HARD? ISN'T 'GOOD ENOUGH' GOOD ENOUGH??"

Nope.

For a long time I liked getting away with being less, with doing mediocre work.

Where are you attempting to get others to agree to be less in the name of you getting away with being less in your own life? Where are you picking apart others (silently or not so silently) when they are shining brightly?

— 5

Leadership in Illness

by Carolyn

"If I could stand here right by your side, that would be enough."

Hamilton

My mom lives in New York, and she's in Los Angeles for one night on her way to Mexico for a vacation. My ten-year-old daughter Lucinda and I are meeting her at the hotel for dinner before she heads off on the next part of her trip. My mom is wildly independent. She's been a world traveler for years and years. She's headed to Mexico because it's January, and living in New York she naturally wants to be in warm weather. My dad is back in New York, because he's not much into traveling and he says he likes the winter. (Umm, really?)

Not long before dinner, my mom texts me from her hotel saying she fell and that it really hurts and she might need to see a doctor.

I immediately downplay it inside, thinking to myself, *It's nothing. She's overreacting. It will be fine, it's probably a bruise.*

My mom is eighty-three years old, and she's pretty hearty, even though she's slowed down a bit in the last few years.

We get to the hotel, go up to her room. She's lying on her bed, not looking great, and I am not sure what to do. Maybe if she ices it, she can get on her plane tomorrow? I'm of course thinking of the impact of her being delayed on my own life as well, much less the complications for her trip.

Little do I know what's to come.

She moves on the bed, trying to get herself to the edge, and lets out a shriek of pain. NOT a small one.

"Grandma/Mom stop moving!!" my daughter and I both shout at the same time. Not in a kind way, but in a "You're freaking us out and it looks really bad!" kind of way.

(Yes, my daughter is picking up some of my less attractive ways of responding to things).

I say, "I think we need to get this checked out, Mom. We need to find out what's up." She says okay, and I call downstairs to the front desk. They tell me that in this kind of situation they have to call the paramedics and get my mom to a hospital. I say okay.

Now we are in new territory.

I'm remaining calm, asking for assistance inside myself, not really sure what's going to happen. My husband John is out of town for a week for work. I keep thinking, *This will all be resolved, right? Maybe she just bruised it badly?*

Paramedics come, bringing with them lots of questions, all of which my mom answers easily—although initially they ask me, as if Mom is incapable of answering them.

(That's a whole other chapter—how people start treating older adults like they're four-year-olds, instead asking their adult child questions before determining whether or not the older person is capable of responding. My parents are fiercely capable of answering all questions about themselves, their health, their medications, their insurance, and so on. My spot coaching here? Ask the older person first; assess their capability before turning to their adult child.)

Next thing I know we're on our way to the hospital in an ambulance. I was very determined to get Lucinda and I into the ambulance with my mom, even though the paramedic asked me if it wouldn't be better to drive separately so I had my car. Part of me wanted to stay with my mom, but another really didn't want to miss the chance to let my ten-year-old ride in an ambulance.

(It turns out to be less exciting than I hoped. No siren—because it isn't an emergency—and Lucinda is underwhelmed.)

We enter the hospital world, which is basically an alternate universe. A world where time changes, the rules are different, and you are ultimately relying on nurses to move the process forward. It's a world where how you show up with a nurse can change the course of your reality.

I used to be very uncomfortable in this environment. Queasy, even. I would avoid it if at all possible, like a child avoids something she's afraid of. I'm not judging myself, just being accurate.

But because of Michelle I had come to know this universe well. Because of Michelle and our relationship, I became someone who knew how to be in this world, someone who could move through it with acceptance and, yes, even leadership.

Because that experience with Michelle was so vital, what I would like to do now is interrupt the story of my mom and share my experience of being Michelle's best friend and business partner when *she* was in the hospital. Because even then she was coaching me, preparing me for what was to come in my own life. My experience with her didn't just help me with my mom when she broke her hip. Even more deeply, Michelle lived out the answer to the question this book asks: what if this is the fun part? I hope that in sharing this story with you, you'll start to see how you can answer that question for yourself.

~

Michelle in the Hospital

I was not prepared to lead in illness.

When Michelle was diagnosed with cancer for the second time, I did not know what this would mean.

I remember exactly where I was when I received her voicemail telling me that her numbers were up and she needed to get more tests done.

All of a sudden everything changed. Again.

This was December. By February, Michelle was in the hospital for the first of what would turn out to be a number of hospital stays.

I did not know what these hospital stays were going to require—of Michelle or myself.

NOT a Hospital Person

See, I wasn't really a "hospital person" before this. The smells, seeing people in hospital gowns . . . not my wheelhouse. Hospitals made me feel strange and vulnerable—and they gave me the creeps.

But during Michelle's first hospital stay, it became clear that she was going to need support.

No, I was not the one who saw this. It was another friend who texted me and said, "She needs people with her. The nurses aren't around enough." This friend was not a fragile or dramatic person. If she was the source of this information, the only appropriate response was to make it happen.

So, that's what I did. Right then, I started working my phone, finding people who would come be with Michelle in the coming days, scheduling them around her husband Scott's time with her, and my own visits.

My Night

Given the timing, I knew we weren't going to have coverage on the night I got my friend's text. I knew that that night was mine to do. Best friend and business partner = this night is yours.

Stay overnight in a hospital with someone? What do I do?

I asked my non-fragile friend. She was a "hospital person."

She said, "Make sure her needs are met. Hold her hand. Do whatever. If she's uncomfortable, get the nurses."

I asked another friend whom I respected. "Ask inside for support. Be with her. You'll know what to do."

I said to my husband, "I'm a little scared. This isn't something I'm good at."

He said, "You'll be okay." He's really good in hospitals—with all medical things, actually, especially when it's for someone else. We laughed a little as I walked out the door in my sweatpants, with my blanket, toothbrush, a book and other stuff in a bag. I knew this was not going to be a good sleeping night.

Michelle had just had a surgical procedure that day, so when I got to the hospital she was a bit groggy and not all that comfortable. She was happy to see me, though.

"I'm here," I said, and we both kind of laughed. Michelle knew that this wasn't my wheelhouse. But she also knew that I was extremely coachable. I was willing. And I loved her, and she loved me. Being together made even this bearable.

I was wildly unprepared for that night. Michelle was uncomfortable and her pain seemed to be getting worse. I kept letting the shift nurse know. But the nurse was concerned about Michelle's blood pressure and didn't want to give her any medication stronger than Tylenol—which was useless. I kept asking the nurse and then telling Michelle what she said in response.

The nurse was getting irritated with me.

Michelle was getting irritated with me.

This was not a fun scenario, and it was getting less fun by the minute.

Not a Clue

I didn't know what to do. I saw the nurse as the authority based on her title and badge, so I said to Michelle, "Look, she's not going to give you more pain medication. We're going to need to ride this out. I'm going to help you do this."

Michelle looked like she wanted to punch me. She was exasperated and in pain, and here I was suggesting to her that we meditate and ride it out. She looked at me with an expression that said, "Are you serious?"

Oh, but I was. Seriously sweaty, scared, uncomfortable, and out on a limb . . .

So we meditated. I played the guided meditations on her phone, I assisted her with breathing, and the grumpy nurse came in every so often. I felt like I was being a "good hospital person."

We rode out the night until the first light of sunrise, Michelle sleeping in little bits, still in pain, while I talked her through it.

Early in the morning, a friend came to relieve me. I let Michelle know I'd be back later that day. I told her I loved her.

I learned later that after I left, Michelle's doctor came in to see her. When she asked Michelle how she was doing, Michelle shared what had happened overnight with the nurse not giving her more pain medication.

The doctor immediately called in the nurse and said, "Don't ever do that again. Ever. If someone is in pain, you call me. I don't care what time it is. There's always something we can do."

I'm no Shirley MacLaine . . .

When I returned to see Michelle the next day, we talked about how she was doing, who was going to come support her, and what had happened the previous night.

She looked at me and said, "I was so pissed at you! SO pissed!!"

"What?" I said, genuinely confused. "I did everything . . . I tried with the nurse, and then I thought, let's focus on just getting you through the night!"

Michelle said, "Where was the Trudy [my mom—a fierce person] in you? Where was SHIRLEY MACLAINE??

I was stunned.

"You mean Shirley MacLaine from Terms of Endearment, when she runs out in the hospital hallway and screams, 'Get my daughter her x!$×@% medicine! SHE'S IN PAIN!'?"

"YES!!" said Michelle

I thought I had done well.

According to Michelle, not so much.

I spent a lot of time looking at this. First, all of the self-judgments: judging myself as not taking good care of my friend, judging myself as an idiot, a loser . . . and so on.

Then I looked at it in terms of what had stopped me from pushing back more with the nurse. Why didn't I say, "Call her doctor! Call her doctor right now!"?

Context

I didn't know I could assert myself in that context—the hospital context. Despite having seen Shirley MacLaine in Terms of Endearment, and despite my own mother having very little regard for most authority figures, I didn't even think about challenging the nurse. I had wanted to be "good." I didn't want to make the nurse mad. As if the nurse being angry with me was the worst thing. Worse than my best friend being in pain. Worse than my best friend looking at me over the course of seven hours with desperation and disdain (not a fun combo, FYI).

It was all a complete and total unknown: the nurses' uniforms (and attitudes), the machines beeping . . . It all left me feeling meek and bowing to the medical authority. Plus, my emotional state wasn't great.

I was in a vastly new territory.

I felt very "less than"—and not at all in my own leadership.

So I learned. A lot. Eight hospital stays later I was, if not a pro, at least no longer willing to accept what anyone said—doctor or nurse—at face value. While not Shirley MacLaine, I was willing to ask more questions. I was willing to push more for pain meds. I was willing to walk out into the hallway four, five, six, ten times and say, "Michelle's not doing well. Can you come in here? Now?"

And I learned that if I was ever unsure, call the doctor. I could always call the doctor.

I dropped the attachment to being liked by the nurses and doctors. I dropped the story that they knew better than me that it was not okay to ask, and then ask again, and ask some more.

I was kind and professional, and sometimes teary and emotional, and sometimes firm and unyielding. None of it mattered anymore.

How About You?

In what context do you disappear?

You, the one who knows how to lead? Or you, the one learning to lead?

Or are there a number of contexts where you "go away" and forget who you are? Or, because you are new to leadership, you shy away from stepping into a leadership role?

For some women, it's when it comes to their finances. For others, it's at their children's schools. Then there's within your own family, with your partner, or your children. And there's always your own health . . .

Why This Matters

When I am coaching someone, it's not unusual that during the course of a six-month or year-long engagement they are faced with a new unknown in their lives. Sometimes it's personal, as in a parent or sibling is suddenly and seriously ill. Other times, it's professional: getting fired, or being faced with a serious challenge (like someone who reports directly to you who is suddenly dealing with an addiction—both have occurred with my clients and myself).

Like me at the hospital, they are suddenly in wildly

uncomfortable territory, having difficult conversations at levels they never previously imagined, or looking someone they love in the eyes, knowing that they might not be here much longer. Or maybe they simply find themselves in an environment that is not "comfortable"—hospitals, jails, three-star Michelin restaurants . . .

No matter what occurs in our lives, we are at times going to be thrust into the unknown. It's a certainty. I don't attempt to "get ready" for this anymore, although when I was younger I had a magical belief that if I imagined a situation enough (my daughter being born, Michelle dying, my parents dying), this would "prepare" me, and it wouldn't be so "bad" or "hard."

It's not true.

There's no amount of imagination that can prepare you for the life events that really matter. What can assist, though, is having a life context, a framework for your life where you "put" everything. For example, my life context is that everything that happens is for my learning, growth, and upliftment. Everything, including all manner of life events that I didn't plan on.

At a minimum, everything can be USED for my learning and growth. (Though it may take time for the upliftment with some things.)

I don't attempt to get my clients ready for the unknown. That's a control tactic. I work with them to develop their own life context (although you can't really go wrong with "everything in my life is for my learning and growth"—it's hard to mess that one up). And I work with them on developing inner strength—the inner strength to know that they can handle whatever comes their way.

Note: I didn't say that they—or I—have to like everything that comes our way. And we don't have to understand it either (understanding is highly overrated). We don't have to know HOW to go through something. We only need to know that we can, and that we will be supported in ways we can't even imagine after we take our first baby steps into the unknown.

Back to the HIP STORY

Within our first hour at the ER a fantastic male nurse turns to us after an x-ray and says to my mom, "You've fractured your hip. You aren't going anywhere. You need an operation in the next twenty-four hours."

I look at my mom, who's slowly grasping this.

I'm still slowly grasping this.

Together we face the nurse, and I say, "Are you serious?"

He replies, "Oh, yes, I'm serious."

"Mom," I say, "I think your Mexico trip is off the table."

"No kidding," she replies.

She is in a LOT of pain, and the nurse gives her morphine for it. I immediately start texting my friends with an update, asking for loving and light to be sent to us.

(If you're asking, "What is THAT?" basically it means PRAY FOR US, PEOPLE! The shit is hitting the fan! We are in a BIG situation!)

I also ask for any thoughts on the hospital we're in, because I don't know the answers to some important questions. Like, is this a good hospital for hip-replacement surgery? This tiny community hospital in Marina Del Rey?

My friends start doing their work. One of them knows the hospital—even knows someone who works there. Other friends call people they know. Meanwhile, my mom is slowly absorbing this.

My dear friend, Amy Hruby, has picked up Lucinda, who is now in her own world, a world of, "My dad's away, Momma is with Grandma: SLEEPOVER!!"

Now it's just me and my mom. I am texting furiously, looking at her occasionally, figuring out what we're going to do. I'm slowly coming into the reality that my week without my husband is not going to look the way I thought. I am trying not to be bothered by this, but it's not working.

Bye-bye week alone with the TV shows I want to watch . . .

Bye-bye dinners thrown together without a thought of what anyone else wants . . .

Bye-bye alone time.

Bye-bye gym.

Bye-bye any semblance of my life.

Hello, HIP REPLACEMENT LAND. Hello HOSPITAL TIME

I instantly know I am going to need to stay at the hospital overnight. But because of Michelle I am, while not a pro, at least a soldier. I know what to do. I know that the nurses won't be in the room 24/7, and my mom will need someone there.

I call my teachers and friends, Drs. Ron and Mary Hulnick, at home, around eight in the evening. They are the BIG GUNS, the people I call when it's spiritual-assistance time. They were the heads of the Spiritual Psychology Program at USM. They developed the program, taught it, and have been in the "transformational business" for over thirty-six years. They are the ones who receive almost all the credit for my awakening into a more mature, compassionate, internally referenced human being having a spiritual experience. (My husband can take some of the credit, as can I.) I have known them since I walked into the classroom at the age of twenty-nine. I worked for them for over twelve years, and after that they asked Michelle, Steve Chandler and I to develop the University's Soul-Centered Professional Coaching Program with them—so I ended up teaching at the school that changed my life (more on that later).

Ron answers the phone. I choke back my tears and tell him what's happening, and he says, "Wow, okay. What a thing." We talk for a few minutes. He lets me know he'll tell Mary and that they'll be sending light (BIG guns = BIG light, which is essentially lots of love) and we hang up.

I feel a little better, although, not as much as I'd hoped. I like things to happen really fast.

We eventually get into a room. My friends tell me that there's a good ortho team at this hospital—no need to go anywhere else.

Okay, at least that's handled. Because I had NO IDEA how I was going to get her to a different hospital.

My mom is fairly drugged up on morphine, but she's still in pain. A nurse explains to her, "You have a broken hip. Morphine isn't going to erase the pain. It will take the edge off." This makes sense, but wouldn't it would be nice if the drug *could* completely remove the pain?

For the moment my mom is okay, so I go home to get some stuff dropped off for Lucinda at her sleepover (clothes for school, teddy, etc.) and to get my own hospital sleepover stuff: sweat pants, a pillow, a blanket. When I get back to the hospital it's clear that my mom only sort of knows I was gone. The nurse looks at me like I'm a little crazy for staying; she doesn't know what I know. I know from Michelle that there will be moments in the middle of the night when you need a new swab for your lips, and the nurses don't come fast enough.

I settle into a longer chair that sort of tilts back and which is not totally horrible. My mom is pretty out of it. She's needing something to wet her lips. We are now in pre-surgery time, so no water, no food, no nothing until surgery—and she's not on the schedule until 7:00 p.m. the next day.

That's right: she didn't have dinner, then this happened, and now no food and water for more than fifteen hours.

I will spare you all the specific details of the next twelve hours. It's a lot of dabbing of lips, my mom being really uncomfortable, me sort of dozing and then hearing her call me, getting up, walking out into the hallway and getting a nurse, getting more swabs for her lips, lots of praying . . . and repeat . . . Again and again and again, until morning light trickles through the window.

Then we do it again for another seven hours.

Somewhere in there I call my dad and brother in New York, and text various people. One of these is my husband, who is on a television shoot and consequently not very available. The former me of five to ten years earlier would have really struggled with him being gone during this big thing. She would have felt abandoned and angry. She would have identified as a victim. "You should be here. You should fly home immediately. You are not showing up for me the way you SHOULD. You are a CRAPPY HUSBAND."

But the current me is really clear: he's at work. That's his commitment—to be there and do his job as a television stage manager. What's more, it's an unusual and major gig: the Superbowl. So he is out of town and has a lot of work to do. There's little time to talk, except here and there.

Don't get me wrong: I would like him to be with me. His support and assistance would be great . . . and I am also a full, mature adult who is okay with how this is all unfolding without him here.

The current me is pretty fine with that.

I'm less sure about how my mom is doing.

The Next Big Thing

My mom finally dozes off after an early morning dose of morphine. I go get real food and coffee for myself outside of the hospital, then return to her bedside and do some work, thinking, "Okay, we're almost there. Almost surgery time. We're doing okay."

The surgeon comes to meet me, and we step outside the room. Dr. Smith is probably thirty-five. He appears nice as well as smart (which seems important for this). He starts to tell me about the surgery.

(Now *I'm* the person who gets talked to about surgery for my mom—which is simultaneously fine and a little strange. Because I realize I am now in FULL adulthood, and it's not lost on me how much I am not prepared for this. Although, having walked through my best friend dying helps. Growing up on many levels happens when these things occur.)

The surgeon talks about how at age eighty-three, things can happen. Statistics show that older people sometimes die within the first year of hip replacement after a fall. Or they don't recover to their previous level of health, instead becoming bedridden, and so on.

I'm watching him as this information enters my sleep-addled brain. Finally I ask, "Wait, what? Die? From a hip replacement?"

He slows down a little, his tone sounding a bit more reassuring as he says, "Yes, and—well, your mom was active prior to this. She was on her way to Mexico. She sounds like she'll be fine. It's just my job to give you all the information."

Well, thanks, I immediately say inside.

Then I think to myself: *deflect*. Deflect is a way to remind myself NOT to take on a thought as "true." For example, "She's going to die." I add, *He's just doing his job Carolyn. Don't take this in as "this is what WILL occur."*

"Let's go inside and get your mom up and ready for the surgery."

She's still sleeping. I whisper, "Mom, wake up. The surgeon is here."

No response.

I say a little louder, "Mom, wake up! The surgeon is here."

He helps out. "Gertrude, this is Dr. Smith. Time to wake up for your surgery."

No response. I'm feeling slightly nervous.

Dr. Smith looks at me. "Does your mom usually not wake up like this?"

I say, "No. She wakes up easily!" I lean over my mom and shake her arm. "Mom," I say with increased urgency, "You need to wake up! It's time for the surgery!" I keep saying some version of this, shaking her, as panic creeps in ever more quickly.

"Don't shake her," Dr. Smith says.

I pause and look at him, laugh and say, "Shaking isn't a good idea?"

He laughs gently too. "No, probably not." Then he pricks her feet with a special tool. When this doesn't get a response he drapes a cold washcloth over her forehead.

No response.

Dr. Smith says, "Let's step outside. I'm going to get the nurses. We need to see what's going on."

Now the slow-motion movie begins. The movie where I am asked to leave the hospital room and the nurses all come in. He and I stand outside, and I'm starting to get emotional—which essentially means that tears are leaking out of my eyes.

Dr. Smith says, "I'm sorry . . . Do you remember what I was saying to you before we went into the room?"

And it hit me. "Oh, my God. You said things like this can happen after a fall, when you're old. Holy crap. It's happening."

"Let's wait," he says. "It's not happening yet. We don't know yet." He pauses, then adds, "We're getting out of my purview here— and I don't do well with crying girls, so . . . We need to see what's going to happen. The anesthesiologist would probably tell us this is because of the morphine. She may come out of it. It could be nothing. Don't throw all your cards on the table yet. You don't know what the other person is holding. She could have aces."

My first thought is, *Crying* girls*? I am a fifty-year-old* woman. *I look good, but I'm* not *a girl—not even close.*

I laugh, though, because I like everything he said. And because I can't leave my coaching out here, I say, "Umm . . . you're in a job where being able to be around crying people is important. And, thank you: I appreciate what you're saying. I won't throw my cards on the table yet."

We go back into the room, where lots of nurses are all trying to figure out what's happening. They're all wearing "we-aren't-sure" looks. I'm crying, and I suddenly realize—and then say out loud— "She's DNR. She's DNR."

They look at me and say, "She's DNR?"

"Yes, she's DNR, do not resuscitate." I am very clear. Crystal clear: if she's done and she's leaving, *don't stop it*. She's eighty-three. It's what she would want—and it's what I want if it's her time.

An older nurse says to me, "How old is your mom?"

"Eighty-three."

She says, "I understand. I'm seventy-three and I've told my children, 'If you resuscitate me, I'll kill you.'"

We laugh. They ask me if they can run tests, and I say fine—only if it's to see what's happening.

Dr. Smith leaves, but not before checking in with me again and letting me know he'll be back to see what's happening. He is my new favorite person. He maintains excellent eye contact with me, he's kind, he's not avoiding my emotional expression, and he's funny. And I am thinking that I will need to invite him to sit with me—meaning "have a coaching conversation with me"—because he cannot walk around saying he doesn't do "crying girls" in his work.

~

Surgery is not an option for the time being. That time has come and gone, and now it's Tuesday night. My mom broke her hip on Monday afternoon. The best window of time for surgery is within forty-eight hours of the break, because of factors like healing time. Tests show no strokes or anything else that might be keeping her from waking up.

I'm thinking, *She needs to come out of this if she's not dying.*

I wait. A few close friends come and sit outside my mom's room while I cycle in and out of it. I talk to my dad, who's getting ready to board a plane, and to my brother Paul, who is holding, waiting to see what happens. Making these calls, saying that we might be in a very different situation than what we'd thought when she first fell—and that she might not make it—is not easy. And I do it.

Over the next ten to fifteen hours my mom slowly comes out of her morphine-induced "sleep."

It takes more time for her breathing to get into the normal range because of her COPD. (Note: COPD and morphine do NOT mix, which we did not know. Now we do. Don't ever let someone give you or your parents morphine if COPD is an issue. This is what created the challenges).

My dad is on his way, because I need assistance—and sleep. This is where being willing to ask for help comes in handy. It's one of the primary things I work with clients on—in particular women clients. Highly accomplished people who are extraordinary at what they do—so much so that to them asking for assistance seems like a weakness in some way. It's a great gift to finally see that it's the opposite: being able to ask for assistance is a strength.

She's ALIVE—Now What?

Of course, we're not out of the woods yet. Now we have to get her back on the surgery schedule. So still no food, no water, no nothing. My mom doesn't know what's been happening; her sense of time is all skewed and she's sort of wacked out, although she's now more awake and able to talk.

It was a long ten to fifteen hours.

She gets back on the surgery schedule for 7:00 p.m. Wednesday night. If you know about surgeries, then you know that the word on the street is you want to be the first in the day to be operated on—not the last. Earlier = more awake surgeons, nurses, and so on. But beggars can't be choosers, and this surgery is happening Wednesday night.

My friend Amy joins me and we walk my mom to the procedure room, giving her a pep talk before she goes in. She's laughing a little and seems pretty okay. Dr. Smith is performing the surgery. I ask him, the operating room nurse and the anesthesiologist—all of them men—if they're awake and ready.

The anesthesiologist smiles at me. "We're excited! We love this."

Mom is wheeled in. I walk into the waiting room to sit with Amy and to send light (pray).

LONG STORY, right?

Surgery is successful. Dr. Smith comes out to talk to me, Amy and my nephew—my mom's grandson, Chris—who has joined us.

Dr. Smith says, "The surgery went well. She's all set. But her fracture was a little more complicated than it might've been. If it had been a typical break, she'd be walking again in a day or two. But unfortunately your mom isn't going to be able to put any weight on her leg for another two to four weeks. After that, she can start walking again."

My face must betray my shock.

Dr. Smith nods. "I know. Your mom is going to be in L.A. for a while. You'll want to find a rehab place for her, and she'll have to have lots of physical therapy. No weight on it, though, for two to four weeks—remember. Then walking from there. She'll probably be in the rehab phase for at least eight weeks."

Still feeling stunned, I say, "You mean, she can't go back to New York for *eight weeks*?"

He laughs and says, "Yes, that's about right."

Holy Mother of God. Bye-bye, current life.

Hello, new project.

My Mom Convalesces in Los Angeles

Some helpful information for you, dear reader. Trudy, my mom, is not known for being easy, accommodating or cooperative in most circumstances. She doesn't deal well with pain or discomfort. She doesn't deal well with not having her way.

She's amazing, and she's one of the most difficult people I know—someone who complains a great deal and who has little tolerance for small annoyances, let alone situations like having her life uprooted and being in a strange rehab facility with lots of OLD people who look to be one step away from dying.

My husband is still away. I have slept little. And I need to find my mom a rehab spot where she can live and recover in Los Angeles. I have NEVER DONE THIS BEFORE.

Again, the adultness of this is on me.

However, what I know now that I did not know before partnering with Michelle is that I can do it.

I can. Even if I'm afraid, unsure, feeling too young (despite my fifty years) and feeling small, I know I can. My capacity has expanded tremendously in terms of my ability to handle hard things. That's one of the benefits and gifts of walking through something very, very difficult: if used properly, it can deepen you and grow you.

I say "properly," because it is a choice. I am part of a grief group on Facebook. I respect each person in there, and I can at the same time see that it's possible to turn away from life for a long, long time. Some visit the Island of Grief longer than others. That's totally natural, depending on the grief. Losing a child is totally different from losing a business partner and best friend. Losing a spouse is different too. So I'm not saying that anyone's length of time is "wrong," just that at a certain point there is still a choice to turn towards life again, even slightly, as a starting place.

My context for life is a big help here. My context, remember, is that everything that happens in my life is FOR me, for my learning. My training at USM prepared me for hard things, for how to at least hang on (sometimes by a thread) to the knowing that everything is for my growth, and that we are divine beings having a human experience.

Back to my mom.

I do the best thing I know how to do, and that's to call Amy again. She is one of the most competent, practical, and solid people I know. She's also deeply caring, wise, and loving. She's a fantastic coach, mother, event producer, wife—and dear friend to me. She's also a second mother to my daughter, Lucinda, and my husband, and I would trust her with anything.

So she's the person I reach out to and say, "I'm going to need your help finding a rehab facility. Will you help me?"

To which she responds, "Of course."

The hospital gives me a list, with four places circled. I give Amy the names of two of them, and she goes to check them out while I'm at the hospital with my mom. My mom is slooowly coming out of the anesthesia. This means she's still pretty wacked out. She tells me several times that she's getting up and going to the kitchen to get soup. When I tell her she can't do that, she gets angry at me.

"Why do you have to make such a big deal about everything?" she asks me, obviously irritated. "I'm going!"

I call the nurse, because I'm not sure what to do here. Do I argue that there's no kitchen to go to? What's the protocol here?

I ask the nurse for assistance. (This is important: ask for assistance). The nurse gives EXCELLENT coaching. "No, don't argue. Affirm reality—as in, 'Mom, you're in the hospital. You just had hip replacement surgery. There's no kitchen to go to.'"

Got it.

Now, my mom has still barely eaten. Because of the COPD and the morphine incident, they won't give her solid food until she's demonstrated she can swallow easily. She's basically eating a little applesauce and some really bad coffee that's been thickened slightly to make sure she doesn't choke on it.

FUN TIMES. I am both concerned and attempting to stay present to the fact that she has an IV in and isn't starving to death. But it's not fun to watch her so desperate for real food and real coffee. She's mentally unclear, too, because of her pain meds and the after-effects of the anesthesia. I catch myself starting to jump into my future, thinking that finding a rehab place is going to be . . . HARD.

So, I do what I know how to do when I'm scared, not in my right mind, feeling low, a sense of being unmoored. I ask inside, and I also start texting, asking for loving and light to be sent to ME (remember, just pray for me, or think good thoughts for me, or send any sort of kindness my way—that's all it is).

I slow down. I remember that assistance is all around us—and that I just need to ask.

My dad shows up. This is good news: I can leave the hospital more often, go home, see my daughter, shower, and sleep.

Rehabs Are Us

Amy visits two rehabs and calls me. She knows that ideally my mom should have her own room, and not in a dark, dingy place that you feel you may never get out of.

Amy tells me, "I think you should go look at [place A], and not [place B]."

And it occurs to me that I actually do have to go look at these places.

OH.

Okay, I'll go. But first I look down the list and see a place Amy hasn't seen, which I think is near our house. I have the hospital call, and they have beds. I ask Amy to meet me so we can see this place together, and then I plan to go look at the other one she recommended.

We go in and we meet with the woman who will show us around. (Note: go to rehabs unannounced. It's how you make sure there aren't people sitting in hallways not being cared for. You want the surprise factor here. This is coming to you from a seasoned pro.)

The rooms seem okay; there are windows, sunlight, and nothing too scary-looking. When I ask about my mom having her own room, the woman tells me that, yes, this is possible, and she takes us to the kind of room my mom would get.

The score goes UP for this place.

Another question comes to mind, so I ask it: "Would you have your parent stay here?"

She looks me in the eye and says, "This is not a fancy place, and it's not new. You can see that." She gestures at the walls, which could use a fresh coat of paint. "The care is good, though, and we are solid. I would have my parent here."

Okay. My inner guidance says this is the place. We go look at one more, just as a reference—one of the places Amy has seen. Not good parking, and it's very busy. My mom would be in a room with three other people. The attendant shows us the activities calendar, but I already know my mom will not be doing social things; that's not my mom. She wants nothing to do with old people who are in rehab facilities—even if she's one of them.

I choose the place with some sunlight and a private room that's only half-painted. It's five minutes from my house.

My Mom Arrives

Friday. Two days have passed since the surgery and the hospital says my mom can leave. I tell her I've found a rehab that's just five minutes from my house.

"If it's terrible," I say, "we'll find a new place."

"Okay," she says. She's looking at me with something like resignation and uncertainty, and I'm aware she's exhausted and hungry. She's on the other side of surgery with a new mountain called "walking again" in front of her. It's not going to happen for at least another two weeks.

I go on ahead to the rehab place. Amy meets me there to help me get my mom's things settled and stowed away. (Amy is amazing, right?) After Amy leaves, I sit in my mom's room, waiting for her to arrive.

And I collapse into deep panic and fear.

My thoughts are: *What if this is a bad place? What if they don't take good care of her? What if one of the nurses jabs her with a needle during the night and kills her? What if they are secretly abusing old people here? WHAT IF?????*

One reason why I am so good at coaching people when they collapse into fear and negative future fantasy is because I know the territory extremely well. I used to be someone who lived this almost 24/7. Now it only shows up in moments of extreme hunger or fatigue, or other similarly over-the-top stressful experiences—and when it does I know how to work with it.

So if you're a budding coach and are thinking, "Me? Coach? I'm a mess!" then know that you can USE your mess and learn how to serve others. This is one of the best things about this profession: my challenges, my blind spots—once seen and worked with—can be used in service to others.

I text my husband, who's STILL out of town. I let him know that I am in a complete panic, and I don't know what to do. He writes two things:

You are doing a great job (heart emoji).

Breathe. Fill her room with loving.

Good texts. I relax a tiny bit. I do what he says.

My mom arrives in an ambulance, the paramedics set her up in her room and the nurses come in to greet her and get her settled. We look at each other, both knowing we have no idea what it will be like moving forward, although my mom has been in rehab once before following a knee replacement. She says she'll know if the place is any good based on the physical therapy she gets. Okay.

A Service Orientation

We spend eight weeks there.

I say "we" even though of course it's my mom undergoing the rehab. But I am usually there two and sometimes three times a day.

Very quickly my mom lets me know that the coffee is horrible and the dinners aren't much better. Within a few days, we establish a morning coffee routine of a double-tall, non-fat cappuccino and some food to supplement the rehab's breakfast, and then dinner almost daily.

My husband is wondering how much all this is costing. I am not (we have different money mindsets).

My nephew Chris becomes part of the rotation. Yes, my twenty-six-year-old nephew says he will come a few nights a week on his way home from work and bring hot tea or dessert for his grandma.

So I am the main person, with support from my husband and Chris.

You might be wondering how I do all of this without stopping the rest of my life entirely.

I serve my clients; that doesn't change.

I take care of Lucinda, although my husband is more on point in this area.

There is no cooking in my house for about eight weeks, other than what my husband does, and I make it clear at the outset that this is how it's going to be.

I go to the gym.

And I build my life around two visits a day.

I become committed very quickly to making sure my mom has things like a weekly bouquet of flowers to make her feel a little better. In addition, I bring whatever else she asks for: shampoo, lip salve, toothpaste, whatever.

What is my biggest takeaway?

Anything is possible with love and takeout.

I learn this because with Michelle I learned that anything is possible with a phone and love. With these two things, I made sure Michelle had someone with her at the hardest times, around the clock in the hospital and at home when Scott or I couldn't do it all or be there. And with my mom, I make sure she has as much comfort as I can muster with a few good meals, decent coffee, my presence, her granddaughter's presence (not to be underestimated—the power of a ten-year old granddaughter), and a rotating list of family members who come out from New York and elsewhere to supplement and support the process. My dad comes three times, for four to five days each time, to relieve me. My brother comes for a weekend, as does my niece, Shannon.

And my husband and Amy. A few other friends are in a text loop, providing words of support and a steady stream of loving encouragement and LIGHT.

Anything is possible with love. I learned what service was at the University of Santa Monica, and how when we serve someone in any capacity (large or small), without any need for acknowledgement or anything in return, it's one of the greatest ways to expand into a more significant level of loving, of gratitude, of an awareness of the preciousness of life. I lived it with Michelle, and it was one of the most profound things I have ever done. Now, with my mom, I experience it again, and it is, in fact, as profound as it had been with Michelle. It changes me, and it changes my mom, and it changes how I relate to her.

I say this to my clients a lot: anything is possible with love.

2018 Daughter of the Year . . . ?

Roughly eight weeks later, after many visits and many trips to an outdoor area behind the rehab building pushing my mom in a wheelchair, she's getting ready to be discharged. Thanks to some intense physical therapy she can now walk with a walker. And soon she'll be getting on a plane with my dad to go back to New York—where there will be more physical therapy, more work, more challenges . . . as she learns to do more for herself again.

She arrived on January 31. It's now April 3. She has wintered in Los Angeles—something she always wanted to do—although this wasn't quite how she had planned it.

We're sitting one last time in this little back area, my mom in a wheelchair, me on a stoop, and we are talking.

"Cara," my mom says, "I've seen everything you've done. All of it. I had no idea you would do this. All your time, all your effort, all the money you spent. The food, the flowers, the planning . . . everything. I thank you."

I'm crying, and I say, "I'd do it again, Mom."

"I see that now, Cara. I didn't know . . . The last time I was sick, I was in New York, and you couldn't be there. So, I didn't know . . . But Cara, at some point I am going to die. Something is going to happen, and I am going to die."

"I know, Mom."

"And, Cara, you need to go on with your life. You can't cry and cry and cry."

I laugh and say, "Mom, I'm going to cry. How long do I get to cry for?"

She responds, "A day. You get one day."

We both laugh, and I say, "Mom, I will go on, and I am going to grieve."

"I know."

I say gently, "Now, Mom, here's the thing. When you get back to New York, and I'm here and you're there, I'm going to call you every day, as much as I can. And there might be a day when I don't call, not because I don't want to, just because things get a little busy, and then I will call you the next day. Will you remember this? I want you to remember this . . ."

She looks down at me on the stoop and says, "Well, I will try to remember, and—human nature being what it is—I might get grumpy again."

(Remember: "grumpy" for Mom is code for "extremely difficult"!)

(And, spoiler alert: she was true to her word. She definitely became "grumpy" again.)

"You can get grumpy," I say, "and can you also just remember this time? Or does the 2018 Daughter-of-the-Year Award have a limited shelf life?"

She says, "I'll do what I can to remember."

That conversation could never have occurred prior to this experience. It could not have occurred prior to my University of Santa Monica education and the presence of John-Roger in my life, or prior to the work of Steve Chandler and his coaching.

And it could definitely not have occurred without Michelle, who showed me through all our time and all our work together, even before she became ill, that loving is always possible. Loving is the thread, and even in the darkest times, it's a choice we can make. There's nothing we can't do that love can't handle. With love all things are possible, and all things are made easier.

Not *easy*; easier.

— 6

Who's Holding Me Back?
Safety and Security?

by Michelle

I have a vivid memory of being nine years old and standing in mid-morning recess at my elementary school. All around me was the organized chaos of children playing with enthusiasm, focus and total absorption. That's usually how I played: totally engaged in my game of foursquare or punch ball.

But for some reason, that day I had a moment where I stopped and looked around. The world froze, time stood still. I was in a bubble of total presence and quiet, while still being aware of the playground cacophony. And I had a thought:

"This childhood thing isn't going to last forever. At some point, the gig of being a kid is going to be up and I'm going to have to go out and make my way in the world."

I knew I lived a privileged, middle-class life. My father was a doctor and my mom stayed home with me and my younger sister and brother. It felt like a stroke of sheer luck that I was born into *this* family and not one living in poverty.

Right there, as I stood between the tetherball court and the kickball diamond, I decided it was time to get real about my life and to begin making plans for adulthood. I didn't want to be caught unprepared or in denial. I wanted to be sure that I remembered I was, in fact, going to grow up.

And from the wisdom of my nine full years of living, I could see only two choices to guarantee that the safety and security I felt in my home continued into my adult experience: I could fall in love and marry a man who could provide me with this life (the choice I perceived my mom had made) . . . or I could earn money myself (and be free to marry whomever I loved, without concern about their ability to provide for me).

In that moment, the second option seemed eminently easier. WAY easier to go out and make money. WAY easier to find someone to marry—if I didn't have to make sure he was also going to be responsible for my financial security.

Because I've always been a fan of the "easy" way, I decided in that moment: I wanted safety. I wanted security. The way to have that was to earn money. And the safest way to be sure you have money is to earn it yourself.

Looking back, I can see that this was a moment of spiritual crisis, of asking deep questions about where safety and security come from. What is the source of protection? How do we feel safe in a world filled with sorrow?

But from my nine-year-old self, this was strictly a question that could be answered by money. So that's how I attempted to answer the question. I put my head down—and I got to work. I did what I needed to do to become financially self-sufficient.

For nearly the next thirty years I lived by that decision.

The decision I made as a nine-year-old colored virtually every subsequent big decision in my life: where to go to college, to go to law school, whom to marry . . . And lots of smaller decisions too:

where to go to dinner, whether to buy a pair of shoes, and so on.

In fact, if you had met me circa 2006, what I would have told you about myself is that I am a risk-averse lawyer. That I am SO risk-averse. That my husband and I are BOTH risk-averse lawyers. That we are financially conservative. That we are risk-averse, risk-averse, risk-averse . . . I probably said this out loud at least once a day—and it probably ran *inside* me hundreds of times a day.

So by 2006 I had in many ways created exactly what my nine-year-old self was wanting. I had a great job at NBC Universal: I was the Vice President of Labor Relations. I had a flexible work schedule so that I could work mostly when my two sons were in school. I had a great husband, a healthy 401K . . . I even had a minivan.

But you know what? I was profoundly unhappy.

I was having the overwhelming experience of, "Is this all there is?" And feeling like everything exciting had already happened in my life. All the big decisions had been made, and now all that was left was to keep doing the same thing for the next forty years.

Truthfully, that thought made me want to gouge my eyeballs out.

I was angry, resentful and bored, and it wasn't pretty. And the people I loved the most—my kids and husband—were getting the worst of me.

Against this backdrop, the University of Santa Monica and Spiritual Psychology entered my life. I dragged my husband to a weekend couples workshop at the University. It proved to be a turning point in my marriage, but even more so in my life. USM is highly transformational and experiential, and as I went through the weekend I had the experience of waking up—waking up to my own dreams and potential—and I LOVED everything about it, to the point that participating in the two-year master's program suddenly seemed appealing.

On a break in the workshop I was walking to lunch with my husband and telling him how alive, engaged and stimulated I felt. I shared how I had wanted to be a therapist when I was in high school, and how I felt like I had missed my calling. I also said I wasn't sure I wanted to continue working in corporate America. I was filled with enthusiasm and talking a mile a minute.

My husband—bless him—turned to me and said four of the most magical words I had ever heard.

"You should do it."

He floored me. That was the last thing I expected him to say.

My response was, "But, honey, we are so risk-averse. And this is such a risky thing to do. I don't know how I can move forward since we're so risk averse."

My husband looked at me with utter puzzlement and confusion, as if I had just spoken some foreign language.

He said, "I'm not risk averse," and proceeded to list all of the risky things he'd done in his life—all of which I already knew. After all, I'd been married to the man for ten years at that point!

And in that moment I saw clearly—perhaps for the first time. I saw that *I* was risk averse, that *I* had been holding myself back, keeping myself small.

No one was doing it to me.

I saw that I had been afraid of life, that I saw life as something to be afraid of, to be protected from . . . and in that moment I didn't much like the results of seeing things that way.

Carolyn:

The thing about all of this is that Michelle moved *fast*. She went right from the Couples Workshop to applying to USM, to entering the program, to being VERY clear she'd be leaving her job as a lawyer (despite enormous fear). She was one of the smartest people I know. The combination of this intelligence and awareness with her growing skillset as a coach, her ability to be with people in their pain, their fear, their discomfort, their dreams—that combination was both fierce and remarkable.

— 7 ————————

Low-Stakes Risks

by Michelle

Often when I talk to groups or clients about adapting a growth mindset, people recognize themselves in my story about being risk-averse. They might intellectually know that taking risks and making mistakes is a good idea, but in reality they avoid doing so at all costs. The discomfort is too intense.

Instead they ask how they can make it less painful for themselves.

I really understand that question. When I knew I wanted to leave my nice, safe, cushy, well-paid corporate job as a lawyer and be a business owner and entrepreneur, I also knew it was going to require me to make mistakes and take some calculated chances. I had to learn a new way to relate to risk and challenge if I was really going to honor my dreams—and give myself the opportunity to go for it.

So I did the most obvious thing: I learned how to knit.

Right. Isn't that obvious?

That may seem like a non sequitur to you, but I had always wanted to learn to knit. Now as you may imagine, making mistakes is part of knitting, especially when you are just learning. And what I saw is that if I wanted to be a really good knitter—if I wanted to achieve a level of mastery—not only was I going to have to make mistakes, I was going to have *deal* with the mistakes.

I couldn't do what I was currently doing in my life, which was just focusing on things I did well and either ignoring mistakes or telling myself they didn't matter.

If I wanted to be a good knitter, I had to acknowledge when I made a mistake and be willing to rip out my work, understand what I'd done wrong, and do it over.

And as part of my knitting experiment I practiced not judging myself while I did it. I practiced instead acknowledging myself for my willingness to learn and grow, and for my progress. The result?

I became good at knitting really fast.

And then dropped it. Now I don't knit at all.

But I'm grateful for what it taught me. And if I can embrace mistakes as a path to learning, so can you. You simply pick any activity as a vehicle for practice: sports are great, for example. It's easier if you pick something you haven't done before, and which is also enjoyable for you—but neither is a requirement.

It is an incredible thing to start consciously tapping into your ability to grow and learn—and to your willingness to make mistakes at the same time.

Carolyn:

So if you are a newer professional coach reading this piece, my invitation to you is to read it again—because mistakes and messy are *the* way to grow yourself as a coach and a business owner.

If you are not a professional coach and simply want to co-create something from nothing (a book, a child, a new job, a piece of art), mistakes and messy are the way to birth that something.

Risk tolerance is a great practice in life. In my experience, anything we really, truly want is risky . . . Or perhaps it only *feels* risky.

In which case, we want to practice doing things that feel risky.

— 8

What Does It Really Mean to Love Ourselves?

by Michelle

When my clients are feeling stuck, or when they're ready to create what's next, there is almost always an opportunity for them to love themselves more. Self-judgment, self-criticism, self-doubt, self-rejection are almost always found as obstacles on the path of growth and greater fulfillment.

One of my clients, a successful entrepreneur and business consultant, expressed extreme resistance to the idea that loving herself more could translate into a different experience of life. In fact, she worried that if she really loved herself, she would get soft and not do anything—certainly not the difficult tasks that her business required.

She wasn't the first or last of my clients to express skepticism that self-love and self-acceptance are key factors in experiencing greater joy and success. Many express hesitation and downright concern, as if more self-love will lead to delusion and denial, as if it is the apple in the Garden of Eden.

Based on these conversations, it seems to me there is a fundamental misunderstanding about what it means "to love ourselves." Somehow my clients equate "self-love" with "letting ourselves off the hook." As if when I allow myself to fully and truly love myself, without conditions, I will no longer work hard or eat healthy. Suddenly it will be chocolate sundaes 24/7 and the mortgage will go into default. Self-love is seen as some hippie ideal with little usefulness or practicality.

With our children we resist the urge to give in to their temper tantrums (at least most of the time) because we know that in the long run it's better for their growth and development. We don't allow dessert before dinner or video games before homework. We do this because we love our kids. We are willing to endure battles of wills with them because we hold sacred our commitment to help them grow—because we love them and we truly want what's best for them.

We love our kids enough to hold a bigger vision for their lives than the one they can currently hold for themselves. We remember what they are capable of when they forget, or when they are too young to see. This is a beautiful demonstration of our love.

Can we learn to hold a similar vision for ourselves? And do it from that same space of deep and authentic caring from which we do it for our kids?

Since when did loving ourselves become about giving in to a momentary desire or collapsing at the first sign of discomfort, rejection or challenge?

Don't confuse self-indulgence with self-love.

Learning to use love as a practical, effective tool (and not just a lofty idea) takes clear intention and conscious practice.

After a year of being treated for cancer, I focused on the process of revamping my health and rebuilding my physical strength. My old way would have been to shame and judge myself into action—as in, "AAAAGH! Look at your body! This is *not* okay. You have to turn the tide NOW before it's TOO LATE!"

I have decades of personal data demonstrating the limited effectiveness of this approach (and the collateral damage of self-loathing that goes with it).

So instead, I now whisper to myself, "I love myself enough to get my body to yoga. I love myself enough to be consistent with my actions without making excessive demands against my body. I love myself enough to resist a bite of clam chowder. I love myself enough to fill my body with foods and experiences that will nurture my health. I love myself enough to keep going even if I make an 'off-track' choice."

I am consciously creating a context of loving and support instead of judgment and deprivation—and I'm not letting myself off the hook. It makes all the difference not only in my experience, but also in my results and my ability to take consistent action over time.

Change the soundtrack in your head, and change your life.

"I love myself enough to . . ."

Carolyn:

Witnessing Michelle take on self-loving in a greater way after her first bout with cancer was both inspiring and uncomfortable.

Inspiring because I saw a new Michelle, a Michelle who was more willing to say no to what she didn't want in service to what she DID want: enhanced health, well-being, peace and ease.

Uncomfortable because it meant she said no to *me* more. No to more work, no to running two groups at once, no to too much email, no to being away from her family as much. This was all appropriate—*and* I experienced it as a step away from me and our work together, which made me sad, even though I was in full support of it. It was an experience of "yes, *and*": yes, you need to say no to this, and yes, I understand, and yes, do it. The "and" part was what I was feeling that I did not express to Michelle, because it would have been asking her to somehow help me with my feelings, or, at a minimum, to acknowledge them. She already had enough work on her hands getting well and taking on her self-care in a different way. She did not need the additional labor involved in taking care of me and my feelings.

I love myself enough to remember how much Michelle loved (loves) me, and to go on, to continue in this amazing life, sharing our work, sharing her, sharing myself, experiencing my own loving for myself, sharing this loving with my family, my friends and my clients, and remembering that life is good.

Life is good.

9

Our Marriages

by Carolyn

Michelle was married; I am married. When we met, we had both been married for a long time by most standards. Michelle and I had both been married for over fifteen years when we first met.

Michelle's husband, Scott, was a fellow lawyer, and someone who for the most part looked on from the sidelines as Michelle and I built our business together. I would see him when I went to Michelle's house for one of our early events—held in Michelle's family room on a Saturday—or at the end of one of our group live days when he and the boys came home. He is one of the smartest people I know, and he has one of the best minds I know.

Back then I didn't know him very well. John and I had one dinner with Scott and Michelle early on, before she started the graduate program at USM, and it wasn't a great one. While we didn't know what had occurred right before we showed up at their door that night, I could feel something was off. That "offness" was

Scott's concern (and then Michelle's) about USM being a cult, and that John and I—clearly cult members, possibly lizards in human skin—were showing up at his home and potentially infecting his wife.

I'm kidding about the lizard part, but he did have real concerns. And Michelle's concerns about *his* concerns were real. I found this out after the dinner, when Michelle and I talked about it. What could I say? As the Admissions Director at USM, the cult question wasn't new to me. USM isn't a cult. (They don't take all your money and they don't ask you to reject your family and friends and only be with other people who are involved at USM. They also don't hook you up to machines and test you on your loyalty or anything else.)

My answer was always the same: "As long as I have been involved at USM, I have never seen or read or experienced anything cult-like. I am from New York—I'm not a cult person. I have a lot of concerns when someone smiles too much, so I know what you mean. I had concerns, too, when I started there. The only thing I can say is that from the moment I entered USM, and from the moment that John-Roger came into my life, only good has occurred."

That was good enough for me. But everyone had to lean into this on their own to see for themselves.

Michelle leaned in. Scott was supportive—and watchful (he's a lawyer). And he was also one of the best sounding boards for our business. Michelle would ask him for his input on how we should structure a fee, or work together, or create our arrangement with USM when we taught the Coaching Program. He would share with Michelle his point of view and his guidance, which was always sound and excellent. And we pretty much almost never took it, although we were very grateful for it. Scott and I laugh about this regularly now.

I mentioned earlier that he eventually became a USM student himself. Scott entered the University ten months after Michelle passed. No cult. He's a different person from the man who warily checked out John and me at his house so many years before. His mind is as excellent as ever, and his heart has expanded in such a way that now many more people get to experience it. His ability to connect, his openness and his warmth have increased exponentially. Michelle used to say that he kept this side of himself pretty exclusively for his family and some friends, and that not many others got to see this. Not true anymore.

Back to our marriages. My marriage was different then because my husband John was a USM grad. By "different" I mean that we had a shared language, a sense of foundation and a context for our lives.

What was not different was that my husband was still a huge source of challenge for me. Despite my USM education, I still made him responsible for my happiness, my unhappiness, and a number of other things. My friendship and partnership with Michelle was the beginning of me unraveling all of that.

What Kind of Partners?

Michelle and I regularly traveled to Steve Chandler's coaching schools as both students and guest speakers—for which he asked us to talk about our work, our stories of leaving our jobs and becoming full-time coaches, and about what it was like to venture into the land of business ownership and the often bumpy, scary, and learning-filled journey to being thriving professional coaches.

Needless to say, whenever we spoke together it was fun—and

funny. We were funny because, well, we were, and because it was way more fun when we were funny rather than upset about the mistakes we were making and the various ways we completely missed the mark with an idea or a prospective client.

On one occasion we were talking with people after the day's sessions were over. One of the coaches who was there came up to us, telling us how much he liked our talks, how much it meant to him to hear us talk as partners about our work and lives, our challenges and so on. Later that night, another person said something similar, and then another.

Something about the way they referred to us as "partners" made me say to Michelle, "Michelle, I think some of these coaches think we are *together*—as in *partners*. You know . . . *life partners*."

She said hesitantly, "Really? I don't think so . . . Really?"

"Yes, I think so."

We laughed. She kept saying, "No, I don't think so." And I kept saying, "No, I think so."

The next morning we went back into the event with Steve, and he pulled us aside and said, "So this morning I clarified for Mike that you are *business* partners, not life partners, FYI."

Cue hysterical laughter.

We made sure going forward to clarify when we spoke that we were each happily married, though not to each other. Not that being life partners would have been bad in any way. And in fact we *were* life partners—just not romantic life partners.

— 10

He Could Leave at Any Time

by Michelle

One of my guiding principles for many years was to seek safety and security. Virtually every decision I made—what job to accept, who to marry, what car to drive, where to live, what to have for dinner—was vetted through this lens. I was serious about my commitment to pain-avoidance.

One of the things I notice about myself (and my clients) is that those of us who are wired to avoid pain like to pretend that we know what's going to happen.

I once had a client tell me with absolutely certainty that she was sad and upset because her parents, who lived on the opposite coast, were aging, and that by her calculations she only had another twenty or so years to spend with them. When I gently suggested that she had absolutely no idea how much time she had left with them, she looked at me blankly.

I knew that blank look. I used to have it all the time. There were certain things I pretended to know, lies I told myself that made me feel better. Those lies protected me from some awful vision of the future that I imagined I couldn't bear. They gave me permission not to worry about that future, not to prepare for it.

One of the biggest lies I told myself was, "My husband will never leave me. My husband will never cheat on me or have an affair."

Now let me be clear: I don't really think my husband is going to leave our marriage or be unfaithful. I have really good reasons for being relatively confident that that's not going to happen. He is an incredibly faithful and loyal person. He has shown up for me in amazing ways every day of our marriage. He is one of the most content, self-affirming, internally validating people I've ever known. His parents had a happy marriage for almost forty years before his mom passed away. Plus, he didn't really love dating back in the day, and he wasn't sure he'd find "the one" the first time around.

But the truth is, I can never really know what's happening inside another human's heart. I can't prevent him from being attracted to someone else or falling in love with them. I can't control whether at some point he has a breakdown or an awakening and wants a totally different life than the one we've created together. I can't defend against involuntary leaving: illness, accident, brain injury.

I can't know what the future holds. But holding on to the lie that I *could*—that he would never leave me—closed down my heart. It gave me false protection from vulnerability. It had me turn my husband into less than the full person that he is. It had me hold him as someone who was a pawn in my need to control my life—by pretending I knew what he would do forever.

Then, during a period of time when he was working very hard and coming home very late, I realized he could be having an affair and I would never know it.

I could pretend he "didn't have it in him," but who was I to say? He could.

When I thought he would never leave me, I had "permission" to treat him as less than a full, autonomous person. I had "permission" to treat his needs as less significant than mine. To see him as less human, less three-dimensional, more fixed in who he is. I could even blame him for the things I didn't like in my life. The fact that I had what I'd always wanted—a good, loyal, decent, dependable husband—meant that I could never "leave," that I was stuck in the life we had created together. It didn't matter that I didn't *want* to leave. This fear was simply a projection of how trapped I felt within myself—it didn't have anything to do with who my husband really was as his own person.

But when I opened to the possibility that he too could have a secret internal life (after all, I clearly had one) and could be doing things that I didn't know about (and there was nothing I could do to stop it)—a space opened up in me . . . a space in which I could be deeply appreciative and humbled by the fact that he *was* with me. I saw that him being in our marriage was an absolute *choice*—one that honored me and our life together. And I could receive that choice as the sacred gift that it was—and unwrap it every day.

I saw that the real opportunity before me wasn't one to take greater control. I didn't need to get my husband to promise he'd never leave me, and I didn't need to lie to myself that I knew he never would. My opportunity was to make peace with uncertainty.

I didn't need to be assured of the future to enjoy the present.

— 11 ———————————————

My Marriage

by Carolyn

For the first twenty-four years of my relationship/marriage, I was still, in subtle and not so subtle ways, operating from the following limiting belief in relation to my partner (maybe you can relate?):

"It's YOUR job to nurture me/love me/tend to my feelings . . . and a lot of the time you aren't doing it right."

Twenty-four years is a long time, right?

And here's the real kicker: I didn't actually know I was doing this. Something felt off, yes. I was feeling not seen by him, not cared enough for by him, not listened to enough, and not paid attention to enough. This became even more pronounced after my daughter was born.

It was painful. Deeply painful. I didn't know if I could keep feeling this pain. I slowly realized I needed to do more inner work, and I needed some guidance. I was not happy about this. My thought was, "I've already done SO much work! Seriously?"

Yet the plain fact was that the birth of my daughter had changed the marriage terrain. Lucinda's presence brought forward material inside of me that had been dormant prior to her arrival. The same was true for my husband. After Lucinda's arrival, I started to feel even more less-than, and second to my daughter in my husband's eyes.

I became more upset and needy in conscious and unconscious ways. At the time I didn't have the words to articulate what was happening, other than to keep trying to tell my husband that the distance between us was increasing, and he needed to "do" something about it.

This was not well-received. Even in our joint therapy sessions, when we were able to have a tentative peace, something deeply unsettling was happening inside me. My husband didn't really hear or see it—he was pretty mired in "baby exhaustion." He was very tired, and angry about being tired. I was tired too, and upset that he didn't see my tiredness as bigger and more important than his own. (I was the MOTHER, after all, and this meant I was automatically more important.)

The Gift of 100 Percent Responsibility

I decided to go back to the University of Santa Monica and audit for a year. I wasn't happy about my decision, but I knew it was necessary for me.

Slowly, over the course of that year, I did a lot of work. I unpacked my inner material one piece at a time and revisited the sad, frightened, little girl who grew up in a house with two unhappily married people. And there, at the very bottom of the box, was the gift of seeing (for the first time) that in fact my husband was *not* responsible for the pain I was feeling.

I was. One-hundred percent.

From this awareness of responsibility, I began to take steps to help this little girl inside of me by updating the old beliefs and learning how to mother myself. I stopped silently wanting my husband to do the repair work instead of me doing it myself. I stopped silently making him wrong for not seeing it. I stopped silently seething inside about who he was and who he wasn't.

I started learning how to SEE my Self. How to LISTEN to my Self. How to PAY ATTENTION to my Self.

How to lovingly, gently, and carefully tend to my vulnerable and afraid places.

I became more willing to be with myself, and more adept at it, and more comfortable with the feelings inside of me. I stopped trying to make John pay attention to me, and I began the important work of paying attention to myself.

What About YOU?

Are you walking around in the world with a subtle or not so subtle assumption that your spouse/partner "should" be there for you when you "need" it? (And if you aren't in a relationship currently, are you thinking as you read this, "Of course they should!"?)

Do you think that if your spouse/partner doesn't ask you how you're feeling at any given moment that this is "not okay"?

If you are single, are you imagining that a relationship will alleviate feelings of sadness, desperation, and loneliness? (It won't. What it *will* do is highlight them in new, not pretty ways.)

Do you make demands (verbal or non-verbal) of your partner (or imaginary/anticipated partner)? Do you have a thought that a partner should in some way "make you feel better"?

Ask yourself this: What does it mean to you to be 100 percent responsible for your own emotional needs?

I have a single client with whom I shared that even though I am married and have a child, I still feel lonely sometimes.

She said in a shocked tone, "Really? Are you serious?"

I said, "Yes, I'm serious." I shared with her that sometimes the loneliness can feel even more stark with a husband and a child in the house. We then started a discussion of what it is to be lonely, and why it's so important to learn how to care for the parts inside that feel lonely.

Important for our own personal growth and development . . . and *critical* if we are going to embark on a relationship that will bring out the unhealed places inside that are yearning for loving.

My Marriage?

My marriage transformed. It is now a place of deep, mutual loving, support, companionship, fun and joy—without the unspoken weight of me silently and not-so-silently attempting to get my needs met by another human being who is doing the best he can to care for himself . . . and who also is doing the best he can to love me and our daughter.

Occasionally I still collapse into wanting my husband to emotionally caretake me. I remember myself a lot more quickly, though, and I can step out of this state with greater resilience. And, interestingly enough, my husband is BETTER at being there for me emotionally, because he doesn't feel me silently "expecting" him to be there. I'm not judging him and making him wrong, so he can relax and be more available to me.

— 12

Welcome Home

by Michelle

At 5:30 every afternoon when I was growing up, my mom would get ready for my dad to come home. She would go into her bedroom, reapply lipstick, fix her hair and make sure she looked good to welcome her husband. Ours was a traditional house. My dad, a doctor, went to work each day and had the sole responsibility for supporting the family financially. My mom did everything else (or so it seemed to me).

Like many girls raised by baby boomer mothers, I was taught to believe I could do anything, and I was told over and over about all the choices I had about who I wanted to be professionally—choices that hadn't been options for my mom.

It was an interesting thing to be given this feminist message and to then watch my mom live a very different life. In a subtle way it felt like she was telling me, "Look closely. Don't choose the life I live— you have more available to you."

My mom loved to shop, and she was always looking for a bargain. I spent a good chunk of my childhood in the Loehman's dressing room in downtown L.A. My mom was a tireless and relentless shopper. She scoured every rack, every nook and cranny for a hidden gem. After a few hours I'd be exhausted, but she was just getting started. (I would always bring a book; I could curl up in the corner and be just fine until she was done.)

The rule in our house was "Never tell Daddy how much we spent—only tell him how much we saved." I remember my mom being so angry at me once when I revealed how much a pair of new boots cost.

For many years, I looked down on my mom's way of doing things. It felt inauthentic. It felt like she was suppressing her rage at the limitation in her life. It felt like she wasn't taking care of herself, wasn't placing value on her own need for support.

When my own kids were young I started to notice the contrast between how I greeted Scott and how my mom had greeted my dad all those years before. Her with her neatly coifed hair and painted lips, welcoming him home with dinner on the table. (It wasn't quite like my picture of 1950s housewives with a cocktail and a dress, but it wasn't that far off.) My dad was put on a pedestal in my house; conversations about how smart he was and how much his patients loved him were routine.

Then we had me: lip snarled, sweat pants on, hair in a scrunchy. I worked three days a week, and because Scott had a much longer commute I was always the one who came home to relieve the babysitter. By the time he walked in the door I was tired, stressed, bored, hungry and angry—or some combination thereof.

I call these "the dark years," because I found the work of raising small children very challenging. I was in a perpetual state of blaming my husband for what I didn't have—but doing it silently, so that there was a low level of rage and blame occurring, but nothing he could see or that we could talk about. So what happened was disconnection.

Then one day I started to wonder what it must be like for Scott to walk into this pit of stress every night after his long day of work, never really knowing what he was going to walk into. I wondered if he looked at me and wished I had lipstick on, or if he would have liked it if I waited a few hours longer to put on my sweatpants.

Would my husband have enjoyed the kind of welcome my mom had given my dad?

The immediate answer was "no"—Scott doesn't care about lipstick, and he wouldn't notice what I was wearing. But I realized I was on to something.

Up until then, when he came home it often felt like an interruption, like he was getting in the way of my flow. If he was late and I had started bedtime, he would disrupt the flow. If I was getting dinner ready he would rile up the kids and make it hard for me to settle them down. It was like he couldn't do anything right.

I had the feeling that coming home at the end of the day wasn't a warm experience for him. In fact, I wondered if he secretly dreaded it, if maybe he intentionally delayed coming home, preferring instead the quiet and relative peace of his office.

I was too afraid to ask.

But I thought I'd try an experiment. What if each night I welcomed him home with a kiss? What if no matter what I was doing, no matter what he "disrupted," I stopped and walked to the door to greet him? What if in my heart I was grateful that he'd come home? Grateful that he was there? Grateful for the extraordinary man that he is? What if I put even the tiniest effort into making coming home something that Scott looked forward to? Would that change things?

I don't know what happened for Scott (because of course I didn't tell him about this experiment), but it changed everything for me. I started see him for the person that he is. I started focusing more on him than myself in those moments, and as a result, my heart opened. I started blaming him less and appreciating him more.

Nancy Kline says one of our opportunities with men is stop asking them to be better than us, to do for us what we are here to do for ourselves. And somehow this is linked to the shift that happened when I stopped blaming Scott and started appreciating him in a deeper way.

Carolyn:

Did you slow down to read this? This:

"Then one day I started to wonder what it must be like for Scott to walk into this pit of stress every night after his long day of work, never really knowing what he was going to walk into. I wondered if he looked at me and wished I had lipstick on, or if he would have liked it if I waited a few hours longer to put on my sweatpants. Would my husband have enjoyed the kind of welcome my mom had given my dad? The immediate answer was "no"—Scott doesn't care about lipstick, and he wouldn't notice what I was wearing. But I realized I was on to something."

And THIS:

"But I thought I'd try an experiment. What if each night I welcomed him home with a kiss? What if no matter what I was doing, no matter what he "disrupted," I stopped and walked to the door to greet him? What if in my heart I was grateful that he'd come home? Grateful that he was there? Grateful for the extraordinary man that he is? What if I made even the tiniest effort to making coming home something that Scott looked forward to? Would that change things?"

Michelle ran this experiment, and as you read:

" . . . it changed everything for me. I started to see him for the person that he is. I started focusing more on him than on myself in those moments, and as a result my heart opened and I just started blaming him less and appreciating him more."

This experiment changed Michelle's life. Then it changed my life.

Michelle's experiment disturbed and shocked me at first. FYI, There was no kissing "hello" or lipstick in the house I grew up in. I want to be clear: my parents loved each other (though they argued often—about money, food, their relationship with each other, their relationships with each of their children). And—there was love there, if you knew where to look . . . complicated love.

After my shock—and, frankly, my disgust and judgement— around Michelle's experiment passed, I decided I WOULD DO THIS.

I decided that if it worked for Michelle, it was worthy—because everything Michelle did and thought, as far as I was concerned, was worthy. My shock and dismay that Michelle would run an experiment and actually <gasp> stop what she was doing and come out of her surliness and KISS her husband and greet him (can you tell I felt betrayed?) covered a small voice inside that said, "Carolyn, this is important. IMPORTANT. Don't miss this."

So I did it. And I do it. Every day, as much as possible. I make a point to kiss my husband "hello" and "goodbye," and to greet him at the door, or to close it behind him as he comes in, to make his homecoming important.

I don't always WANT to, and I do. Because this is who I want to be in the world, in my marriage, in my life. It felt foreign to me for a long time after I started. It doesn't anymore. In fact, now I marvel at who I am.

Michelle shared this experiment in our women's coaching

groups. The responses varied from shock and disgust to intrigue to appreciation to fear and even to outright anger. As in: "What are you, the 'little wifey'?"

She challenged this as only a highly intelligent, heart-centered professional coach and former lawyer could. And she challenged the women in our groups to run their own experiments. We said, "See what happens. Be a scientist in it, and see. You can always go back to grunting at your husband from the kitchen/office/yard and resent his presence when he enters the house. That's always going to be available to you."

So, they ran their own experiments, and lo and behold, many felt what Michelle felt. And many felt what I felt: BETTER, more loving, more connected—and less resentful. Some didn't, and that was okay too.

Run Michelle's Experiment

I invite you to run the experiment whether or not you are reading this with disgust and disturbance. Run it with precision. Keep a daily log. Each day, rate your level of connectedness, or closeness to, or level of appreciation for your husband or wife or partner at the end of the day—"1" being very little and "10" being super high. See what happens.

— 13 —————————————————

Vulnerability

by Michelle

"Worry" used to be a way of life for me.

I was aware from a very young age that I had a privileged life. Compared to what I saw around me and what I read in the newspaper, my life had been virtually tragedy-free. I remember being nine or ten and thinking that everyone was probably going to experience some measure of sadness, of tragedy, of trauma in their life. The fact that my life had contained so *little* of it actually created stress inside me. I figured it was coming someday, and I was truly terrified of what it would be like to walk through some of the tragedies I saw others experience. Would I be able to handle it?

I ruined a lot of days with worry.

The first two days of my honeymoon in beautiful Bali were consumed with worry left over from our wedding: Where did I put the garter I borrowed? Did my Mom still have hurt feelings from a perceived snub from a guest? Did I turn off the toaster?

These worries circled through my mind on a continuous loop until I finally settled down and enjoyed paradise.

My husband loves music and we often go see bands play live. In the early years of my marriage, these concerts became two-hour worry fests. I worried about a case at work, I worried about my marriage, I worried about money, I worried about my sister, my brother, my parents. Every aspect of my life was fair game for worry.

I felt myself to be a total victim of my habitual, repetitive-thinking loop. It would create so much anxiety inside of me that sometimes I'd have to leave the concert to make a phone call or send an email in an attempt to relieve the internal pressure.

In 1998 I was pregnant with my first child, we bought our first house, my husband got laid off from his job, my mother-in-law had a recurrence of breast cancer after three years of remission, my mother was diagnosed with breast cancer and my dad had a benign brain tumor. It felt like this was the year I had been dreading since elementary school. Truly difficult stuff was happening. (Truly wonderful stuff was happening too.)

Of all these situations, my mother-in-law's health was the scariest. Years before she had been diagnosed with fairly advanced breast cancer, and this time it appeared that her body wasn't responding as well to additional treatment.

I was terrified that she was going to die. I loved her very much. And I was so scared about what would happen to my husband, to our family, to his dad and sister if she died.

In my fear, I withdrew. I attempted to protect myself. I didn't call as much as I could have. I didn't visit as much as I could have. I didn't take advantage of the time we had. I was too scared. My worry was an attempt to protect myself from pain, from loss. My worry was an attempt to prepare myself in the event of tragedy.

We gathered together for a family reunion in May, 1999, to celebrate Scott's grandmother's eightieth birthday. My son, Alex, was six months old at the time. It would be the last time we would spend with my mother-in-law.

It was hard to see how tired and sick she looked. She did her very best to be with us; she would come early in the morning to pick up Alex and take him to breakfast, giving Scott and I some time to ourselves.

But she wasn't really able to talk with us about what was happening. We didn't know her prognosis. We didn't know how she felt about living or dying. We didn't know if she was scared or angry.

There was so much that was unsaid.

I wanted to do something for her, to tell her how much I loved her—but I didn't.

Six weeks later she died. It was a shock. We had no idea that she was that close to leaving us.

I was numb as I flew across the country with my eight-month-old infant to attend the funeral.

Her funeral and the days that followed were truly difficult days. Painful. Hard. Bad days.

From that place, I could see that all those days of fear and worry I had engaged in before she died were folly and indulgence. That worry served so little purpose. All it did was keep me away from my mother-in-law—and my family. It kept me separate.

I knew that life was going to contain a certain number of crappy days—really hard, emotionally challenging, truly bad days. This is just part of life.

And I also saw how up until I walked through this very challenging experience—until I had to watch my husband bury his beloved mother just a few weeks after she turned fifty-eight—what a truly crappy day was. It was hard to find any days in my life up until then that could compare.

I knew I had to stop. I had to stop turning perfectly fine, non-crappy days into crappy ones. The crappy ones are hard enough. I didn't need to create more of them than necessary.

When the crappy days came, I now knew I could handle them.

Whatever happened, I would walk through it. And, also, no amount of worry was going to stop the crappy days from happening.

But worry *could* ruin my beautiful life. It could steal opportunities to be close to the people I love, to be present in my life.

Worry is just another name for fear. And, fear had robbed me of so many beautiful days.

It had to stop.

That was my vow. In honor of my mother-in-law, I would no longer ruin "non-crappy" days with my thinking.

In many ways my own spiritual awakening began in this moment, with this decision.

And even with all that was to come—my own cancer diagnosis and treatment, my mom's illness and death—I've had very, very few crappy days since. Even in the darkness, the light is present. Even in the grief, love is there to lead the way. When I focus on the love, I find meaning and strength. I find a way for the day to not be crappy.

Carolyn:

Do you remember back in the introduction? The conversation that Michelle and I had in the hospital?

> Michelle mouthed/spoke/wrote, "If I die, I don't ever want it said that I died after a 'long, hard battle' with cancer. It has not been a battle. I have had joy every day."
>
> I looked at her again and said, "I hear you. No long hard battle with cancer, got it. And—joy every day. Really though? I mean, joy even in this?" I glanced around the room, and pointed at the cards

and paper where we were trying to figure out what she was trying to communicate.

"Yes, even this. This is fun," she said, smiling, looking at the cards.

Michelle wasn't kidding around when she wrote above, "I've had very, very few crappy days since."

She meant it. And she lived it.

I would put together her hospital schedules of people who'd be visiting with her during a particular stay. Sometimes I'd be with her at the hospital and she'd look at me from the bed and ask, "Who's coming tomorrow?" and I would give her the lineup. Michelle would look at me and smile and say, "What a great lineup! That's amazing."

Seriously. She meant it.

And I would laugh, kind of. I would also feel really good that I was doing something GOOD for Michelle. But seriously, who says that about the people coming to be with them when they're in the hospital with a life-threatening illness?

Michelle and I both came from hard-core worrying parents. Like Michelle, I could worry my way to a gold medal—or at least jump out into the future and imagine a movie-worthy worst-case scenario.

One of my favorite quotes about worry is this:

"Worry is atheism put into a socially acceptable slot."

In other words, if we're of a religious or spiritual bent and we walk around saying, "I don't trust the divine plan, I have no faith that the Universe is benign, we are really just like ants, crawling around, scrambling, and then it's over," people might look at us with mild to profound disturbance and wonder, "What happened to her?

Has she given up on life?"

Whereas, if we turn to someone and say, "I'm really worried about my mom. I'm worried about her recovery, and I'm also worried because my daughter is going to sleepaway camp for two weeks this summer. Can she handle two weeks? And I'm worried about our country too . . ."

That person would likely nod and say, "I get it—it's all so worrisome, isn't it?"

We approve of worrying. We accept it as a worthy activity, a worthy use of our thoughts, our time, and our energy.

But worry represents a lack of trust, a feeling that there is no divine plan. So if you have a spiritual practice or observe a particular religion (or both), the next time you start imagining everything that could go wrong it might be worth considering: Are you bowing to the God of Worry?

— 14

Good News: You Don't Get What You Want

by Michelle

I vividly remember my first conversation with Steve Chandler. This was well before he became my coach, but after I had read many of his books. I was in my second year at USM, and part of my second-year project was to interview heart-centered leaders about how to live and lead from the heart.

At the time my most heartfelt and desperate wish was to transition from being a lawyer to a professional coach. And this seemed undoable to me. It seemed impossible that I would ever make as much money as a coach as I did as a lawyer—or that I would have the courage to walk away from my safe corporate job.

In my heart I knew I was a good coach, but I was also a new and inexperienced coach. Sometimes I was over-eager. Sometimes people didn't like the way I worked with them. Sometimes I worried that I wasn't good enough.

In our conversation, I dared to ask Steve the secret question that most weighed on my heart:

"What if I don't get what I really want? How do leaders handle it when there is something they really, really, really want—and they don't get it?"

He said something I will never forget: "If I don't get what I think I most want, that's the best thing that could happen to me."

What?

NOT the answer I was expecting or wanting. I really didn't understand it.

In my confusion, and after a long silence, I managed to ask a follow-up question, which I'm sure was a gargled and inarticulate noise rather than a fully formed question. It boiled down to this:

"Huh?"

Steve responded, "If I don't get what I want, that's the best thing in the world that could happen, because then I get to see that I don't need that thing to be happy."

I was deeply disturbed by this answer. Didn't he hear what I had just said? I really, really, really wanted to change careers. I was really, really, really afraid that I would go for it and fail.

Was he really telling me that failing was a good thing? No . . . Not just a good thing, but the *best* thing that could happen?

The idea was disturbing enough that I knew there was something in it for me, but it would be several more months before I fully understood the power and beauty of what Steve had given me.

Carolyn:

Let's look at this statement by Steve again:

"If I don't get what I want, that's the best thing in the world that could happen, because then I get to see that *I don't need that thing to be happy.*"

I LOVE this. It's a learning context for life in one sentence:

"I GET TO SEE THAT I DON'T NEED THAT THING TO BE HAPPY."

This applies to any of us who are thinking, "That blows. I want my heartfelt dream of marriage/kids/a house/[insert what YOU want here]."

Steve is pointing out to Michelle that our happiness is not an external job. It's an internal one. Our happiness is not dependent on GETTING what we think we want. Our happiness can be chosen and cultivated regardless of what we get or don't get. In fact, our happiness can be about right where we are, instead of where we think we want to be.

— 15

Coaching as Gardening

by Michelle

When I tell people I'm a life coach, they often respond wistfully, with a touch of sadness, "It must be so rewarding to help people." As if to say, "I wish I could have a career where I got to transform people's lives."

I always feel a bit disconnected from this kind of reaction, because it doesn't quite capture the experience of the work I do. Yes, I find what I do incredibly rewarding and fun and challenging and stimulating. But more than "helping people"—as if I were a teacher or a guru or a shrink—what feels more accurate is that I provide people with the space, tools and possibility for them to help themselves.

Coaching, for me anyway, is about providing the necessary ingredients for people to grow into (or wake up to) who they truly are. It's less about what I "do" for them and more about providing the right combination of space, attention, reflection and tools for them to co-create more of what they want, to stretch into more of what's possible for them and their lives.

Being a coach is like being a gardener. Having experience

about what helps plants grow can make a big difference. Being willing to be patient and consistent in providing the best conditions for growth is powerful. Knowing what ground is fertile and ripe for growth—and where the land is fallow and better left unplanted—matters.

But only a fool would say, "It's so rewarding to make plants grow." As a gardener, I am a *caretaker of a process*. A gardener provides the conditions that *help* a plant grow, but they do not *make* the plant grow.

Now, in no way do I mean to diminish the value of the skill and experience I bring to my clients. Similarly, I never take for granted how important my love, acceptance and quality of attention is for my clients' ability to grow. In a sense, the way I am with clients is the way sunshine and water are to a plant. When my clients step into a session, they know that I care about them enough to help them grow, and to tell them what I see as the truth—even if it's uncomfortable.

Of course it would require a true delusion of grandeur to announce, "I make plants grow." No matter how skilled we are as gardeners or coaches, we don't hold the keys to life. We can't force a process that is at its core mystical and mysterious and beyond our ability to control. At best, we are able to participate in something bigger than ourselves. And, when we do it well—with skill, experience and love—the results seems to be better than if growth were to occur without our participation in this special way. Coaching is a generative process: it creates value that wouldn't exist but for these two people coming together for the purpose of creating, growing, and expressing.

This is how it is for me as a coach. I experience extreme reverence for the process I'm invited to participate in. I feel humbled and inspired by my clients' courage and determination. I feel driven to keep growing, learning, reading, exploring my own edge—so that

I have more to share with the extraordinary people who walk through my door. I don't have an over-inflated sense of myself as a "helper." Rather I experience awe in the unfolding process of growth. And I feel excited and honored to be invited in again and again to witness and be a midwife to what often feels like a birthing process.

While coaching my clients, stories—my own and those of others—are some of the most powerful tools I have. Stories open up possibility for people. This is why humans have been telling them since the beginning of time. And we never forget a good one. I find that there are certain stories I tell again and again, ones that really seem to help people in their own growth process. Some are my own stories; others are stories my clients have given me permission to share.

I'll share one here, in the hopes that it will give you more tools to tend your own garden.

~

A man came to me to ask for coaching. He was struggling at work. He had worked for his company for a very long time—really all of his adult life as a father and a husband. And he found himself working for a boss whom he didn't respect, in a situation where the operation seemed to conflict with his own deeply held values. For the first time, he felt out of synch with his company—undervalued and also trapped, scared, and confused. We talked for a long time about what might be possible for him, what he might want to create. And he decided he wasn't quite ready to do the work required to create something different. He decided to stay for the time being.

Six month later he called me. His position had been eliminated. He was disturbed, sad, surprised and scared. I wasn't surprised. I have seen this so many times. We know we aren't where we are supposed to be . . . We have such clarity that what we're doing (a job, a relationship, where we're living) is no longer working for us, and yet we stay, and we don't take action. We've all done this at some time or another. And in my experience, if we don't listen to that inner knowing, our Universe tends to give us stronger feedback—a push, if you will. Knowing this has helped me be more courageous in my own life; I attempt to listen to my own inner guidance before a push is necessary.

I agreed to help my client navigate this new territory, and we began our work together.

The terms of his layoff were very interesting. His position was actually not going to be eliminated for another seven months, and then after that he would receive almost a year of severance pay. So he had a long time to create new employment, but he also had to stay in the workplace for many months. What's worse, they were asking him to stay and help restructure the department, hire his replacement (someone at a lower level) and help train others to make a smooth transition. As his staff found out about his layoff, he had trouble simply receiving their sympathy, and instead spent time deflecting it and reassuring them. He found it all humiliating, embarrassing, and very challenging.

How was he going to stay in this role for the next seven months?

We created a game. I offered to him that he could decide how he walked through the next seven months. We talked about the psychotherapist Viktor Frankl[6] and his book *Man's Search for Meaning*, and how he taught us that no one can take away our dignity and that we have the ability to choose how we walk through a challenging situation.

---

[6] Victor Frankl's most famous book, *Man's Search for Meaning*, was first published in 1946. The book details Frankl's experiences in a Nazi concentration camp during World War II and his subsequent creation of a psychotherapeutic technique called logotherapy.

So how did he want to walk through this? What qualities did he want to demonstrate? What would make him feel good about himself, regardless of outer circumstances?

In other words, we switched his focus from one where he was being defined by outer circumstances ("I just got laid off and people feel sorry for me") to one where he was being defined by his own choices, his own values.

He decided he would practice integrity and excellence. He would get into cooperation with the situation and do his best to support his team and the transition. In the meantime, he would begin the process of reaching out to colleagues and creating new work for himself.

The game began. It was very difficult to sit through meetings in which the restructure was discussed, to talk about how to divide up his job responsibilities, to interview potential replacements . . . But he held fast to his intention: to demonstrate integrity and excellence as he walked through this experience.

And then, a few months into this work, a curious thing happened. He was offered the opportunity to interview for an internal position. He met with his potential new boss and felt an instant connection. This new boss was much more aligned with his values and his focus. She had known him for years, she knew what he was capable of—and she was very excited about him joining her team.

Just like that, he had a new position.

A few weeks later, he attended a meeting with his current boss, the head honcho who had eliminated his position (and who his new boss reported to). After the meeting, my client stayed behind, using the opportunity to shake his old boss's hand and thank him for the new opportunity (still practicing integrity and excellence—this seemed like the thing to do). As the boss shook his hand, he looked directly into my client's eyes and said, "You earned this opportunity by the incredible way you have walked through this situation. I so appreciate how you've handled yourself. I'm so glad we were able to find a position for you so we can keep you working here."

What an amazing thing to witness. A very difficult situation, used properly, gave my client an opportunity to demonstrate who he truly is. Instead of being humiliated and shamed (as he had feared), his willingness to act in a conscious and empowered way gave him the opportunity to show what he is made of, who he truly is.

~

There are things people want that are so universally accepted as things we *should* want, that most of the time we don't slow down enough to inquire *why* we want them.

It took me a long time to understand this as a coach.

If someone should sit in front of me and tell me they want to make more money, or be in a loving relationship, or have children— I would simply agree with them. Of course they want these things. Don't we all? After all, aren't these "good" things to have? The things that matter? The things that really count?

But what I've found is that when I slow down and talk to people there is almost always a misunderstanding about what they want and why, and further—*about what having what they want will do for their lives.*

The compulsion to believe that if I only had [more money, a partner, kids, a better job, success as an artist . . .] I'd be happy seems to be part of the human condition. It's so enticing to believe that external conditions are what make us happy or unhappy, and that if we aren't happy there is something missing outside of us.

It's the ultimate victim position to make something outside of you the arbiter of your happiness. The demands we make against life only serve to keep us separate from the life we already have— with all its bells and whistles!

Carolyn:

I'm left a little speechless by this piece. Michelle articulates so beautifully and with such precision what it is to be a professional coach—the kind of coaches she and I are. This is about coaching from the heart, without attachment to thinking, "I'm the one doing it, it's me"—which is an ego-based reference point. This speaks to the quality of our training at the University of Santa Monica and with Steve Chandler.

My favorite lines are these:

In a sense, the way I am with clients is the way sunshine and water are to a plant. When my clients step into a session, they know that I care about them enough to help them grow, and to tell them what I see as the truth—even if it's uncomfortable.

This is how I felt almost every time I spoke with Michelle, or any time we were working together. Michelle was sunshine and water.

Here's the thing, though: even though I never thought about it until this moment, I can be sunshine and water too. For myself, my husband, my daughter, my clients, my friends and my family. That's my intention. And you can be too. This doesn't just apply to professional coaches, although it's a fantastic way to talk about this work (I use this piece all the time with professional coaches).

Imagine if we all walked around in the world with an intention to be sunshine and water for everyone in our lives. What would occur?

Try it out. It's a worthwhile experiment.

— 16 ——————————————————

We Leap Forward into a New Endeavor

by Carolyn

(Teaching at our Beloved University of Santa Monica,
and the S%$*T Hits the Fan)

(AKA Other big stuff happens, we both grow up and our spiritual
training becomes very, very important)

In 2013, Michelle and I had a conversation with Steve Chandler. He'd been in conversation with our teachers at USM, Drs. Ron and Mary Hulnick. They were talking with him about launching a coaching program for USM grads. He said to them, "The only two people I know who can do this who have both the USM training and the training in my work, who have succeeded in building very strong practices, and who also know how to teach and are excellent facilitators, are Michelle and Carolyn."

That's where it started. Steve said this to Ron and Mary, and then Ron and Mary asked us to talk with them. And that's where the University of Santa Monica's Soul-Centered Professional Coaching Program began.

Who Are Drs. Ron and Mary Hulnick?

A quick note for interested readers: I've mentioned Drs. Ron and Mary Hulnick throughout this book already, but I should give you a proper introduction now. Ron and Mary are the co-directors of the University of Santa Monica, the Center for the Study and Practice of Spiritual Psychology. They have developed all of USM's Spiritual Psychology offerings and have been the lead faculty at the school for over thirty-five years. Prior to their work at USM they were teaching at New Mexico State University; Ron is a licensed Marriage and Family Therapist and Mary is a licensed clinical psychologist. My time as their student was some of the most transformational of my life. Everything to come in my life after being a student at USM was made better because of them and the principles and practices of Spiritual Psychology. Simply put, they are the most loving, effective, and transformational teachers I have ever experienced, and they continue to be very important people in my life to this day.

Teaching at USM

The next thing I knew we were all in the USM conference room with the fabulous Lisa Peake. Lisa would serve as the Director of the USM Coaching Program. It was she who had originally put forward the idea to Ron and Mary about having a coaching program for USM grads, one where grads could learn how to translate their USM education and the principles and practices of Spiritual Psychology into a coaching practice. Steve's role was key in this, because he was already on the forefront of teaching coaches how to grow their businesses in a service-based model, one that relied on slowed-down relationship building.

And we built the program. Ron and Mary brought their years of teaching and developing the principles and practices of Spiritual Psychology to our curriculum meetings. Together we developed a highly experiential, six-month program for USM grads that would assist them in becoming professional coaches serving people using Spiritual Psychology and creating an income doing so.

It was an extraordinary time. The meetings were fun, inspiring and creative. Michelle was FANTASTIC at developing curriculum. I already knew this from the many groups we had developed and co-led. It was even more fun, though, to witness Dr. Mary Hulnick— my former boss of twelve years and first "coach"—experience Michelle's ability in this area. Michelle was a professional. She was very, very good at communicating what would and wouldn't serve these USM grads. Michelle's intelligence, her deep connection to the principles and practices of Spiritual Psychology, and her loving, creative presence was fully *there*—and Mary saw how much she brought to the table in the development of the program.

Privately, Michelle and I were going through our own turbulent time thinking about teaching and being onstage at USM. We were alternately terrified and excited. Ron and Mary would be there, and they'd never seen us facilitate or coach. They knew me well from my time as the head of Admissions and Marketing for the school, and as the spokesperson for the University. Yet they had not experienced me in this new context.

Michelle and I would text each other late at night:

What if they think we're terrible at this?

What if we get up there and start to work with students and they think, "What did we do putting these two up there?"

What if they say, "Get the hell off the stage"—and they have a big hook and pull us off??!!

I of course loved texting Michelle with all the outlandish things I could think of around that—for the sheer enjoyment of it. The reality, though, was that we were both nervous. We were going to be stepping out amongst our peers in a more public way, in a brand new program at the university, sitting alongside our coach, Steve Chandler. Very few people had taught classes at USM without Ron and Mary on the stage alongside them. Those who had were no longer doing this, because the university had stopped offering the Counseling Program where grads could pursue further study to become licensed marriage and family therapists. For many in the community, it was a BIG DEAL that we were going to teach the program—and Ron and Mary were not.

It was a BIG DEAL to us too.

We started enrolling students into the class. Veronica Alweiss, the former USM Admissions Director and now a full-time professional coach based in New Orleans, was the primary enroller for the Soul-Centered Professional Coaching Program. Michelle, Steve and Lisa Peake also did enrolling.

Soon the class was filling up. Conversation after conversation, we were approaching sixty students.

Michelle and I decided that in preparation for teaching six full weekends, one weekend a month, we'd get some new clothes and have our wardrobes looked at by a professional stylist. (USM grad Jennifer Butler did just this.) I warned Michelle, "She's going to make you stop wearing black. She's going to tell you it's not in your color palette." Michelle responded with, "No one can stop me from wearing black if I want to."

We met with Jennifer, we got our colors done—and Michelle found out that black is not in her color palette (she's a Golden Summer, which means no black). She also, in true Michelle form, was thrilled and excited by her new color palette and everything about it.

Earlier that day Michelle had mentioned to me that she might get a call from the doctor because she'd recently had a mammogram. This seemed a little strange to me, and I had to wonder: why did she think she'd get a call unless maybe by then they'd already seen something and it was being tested?

We were at Anthropologie with Jennifer and her assistant, trying on new clothes in our respective color palettes and laughing about feeling like we were in a movie. They were bringing piles of clothes into our dressing rooms. We didn't even have to look at the options on the racks; they just brought the clothes to us.

Then Michelle got a call and stepped out of the dressing room.

I could see her sitting on a nearby couch, and I paused in my trying on of clothes and simply stood there, watching her. I heard her say, "So it is. Okay, so now I need to come in . . ."

And then she started to cry, and I thought, "Oh my God, she's being told there's something there, and it's not benign." I just looked at her as she talked, sending her as much loving as I could muster, feeling myself panic a little. She got off the phone, looked up at me from the couch and said, "The doctor is saying it's cancerous . . ." She said a lot more and I didn't hear any of it, and I don't remember it now. I remember her coming back into the dressing room crying, and me saying, "Let's call Mary and Ron right now. They'll be able to help you." I dialed their home number, and I think Mary answered the phone. Michelle got on.

She cried as she talked to Mary, and relatively soon she calmed down. Mary said a lot to her, and then they ended the call. Then Michelle said to me, "I need to call Scott," and she called him, and she cried again.

After that, she said to me, "Well, we probably should finish shopping."

I said, "Are you sure you want to do that? Because we can finish another day."

Michelle, in her inimitable way, said, "What else am I going to do? We need to get this done, right?"

I said, "Okay."

Because remember: I didn't know what the hell I was doing at the beginning of her cancer journey, so I listened to her. As far as I was concerned, she was in charge.

There's a lot more to share around this. What I will say for the moment is that Michelle decided she'd still teach the program, and she went forward with the initial cancer diagnosis, assuming that this would be a "standard breast cancer" thing, meaning "one and done." Treatment, and then moving on with her life.

As we all know now, that wasn't the case.

— 17

Teaching at USM

by Michelle

Teaching at USM was one of the most exciting and challenging assignments in my professional career.

It was such a thrill to teach subjects so dear to my heart: translating a Master's Degree in Spiritual Psychology into a prosperous coaching practice, and growing in mastery in our coaching.

At the same time, it was such a confusion of roles. I was teaching many people who had been my classmates, friends and clients over the years. I was also teaching as a colleague with my own beloved coach, Steve Chandler, and co-creating and developing curriculum with Drs. Ron and Mary Hulnick, my beloved teachers. What's more, I was facilitating using the principles and practices of Spiritual Psychology with the *creators* of these principles (Ron and Mary) sitting in the back of the room.

Thank goodness Carolyn was on stage with me. At least that was familiar—just as it should be.

And if all that wasn't enough, I was teaching while being treated for breast cancer . . . which required me to walk in front of sixty-four students and a dozen or so assistants with my best wig and barely any eyelashes, feeling varying degrees of nausea and physical discomfort.

I decided not to share my diagnosis with the class for lots of reasons, but mostly because I couldn't handle the scrutiny. I had no idea how I would be feeling and what my energy would be like as I underwent chemotherapy. I didn't want anyone looking at me too closely, wondering if I was "all there." If I wasn't feeling well, it would be easier to "fake it" if no one was paying that much attention.

I learned how to keep calling myself forward, to stand in my professionalism in the midst of these changing roles, to focus on serving the students in the class. As soon as my attention started to drift back to me—"Am I doing a good job? What do Ron and Mary think? Does Steve agree with the answer I just gave? Is Carolyn coming off as a better coach than me?"—my sense of myself would start to crumble . . . and I saw how I could collapse into my insecurities, fears and deep desire to be liked and approved of. When that happened, what kept me going was focusing on the students and what I could offer them, how deeply I could listen to them, and what else I could share.

Ultimately the main thing that helped was to remember over and over again that how I looked personally was of no consequence.

It was a hugely vulnerable experience—and it was fabulous.

It was vulnerable to receive the students' appreciation of the work we did. It was vulnerable to accept compliments on my new "hair." (I have never in my life received so many compliments about how I look! Yikes). It was vulnerable to work with students and coach them with Ron and Mary in the back of the room. It was vulnerable to take center stage and share.

Awkward and uncomfortable come to mind too.

It was also thrilling and humbling.

Here was the best part: when I came home after a weekend of

teaching I would meet my family for dinner. They would text me their location and I would bolt out of the USM building and into my car and fly over the 405 back to Encino, back to the Valley, back home.

One weekend, I remember texting Scott before I left school, "Where are you?"

"We're heading to Menchie's for yogurt"

"I'll meet you there"

I didn't feel like yogurt and I don't like Menchie's (everyone knows Yum Yum Yogurt is where it's at). I was tired to my bones after a full weekend of teaching. But my heart lifted as I pulled into the parking lot and saw those three precious people around the fire pit on the patio.

As I sat in the empty seat they had saved for me, I only half-attempted to follow the conversation already in progress. Mostly I just took in the glory of them. The peacefulness, the comfort, the ease.

Before long, my son Logan launched into filling me in on the weekend. I let his words wash over me—too tired to take them in, but delighting at the sound of him, warmth spreading over me as the professionalism, the intentionality and the demands of the weekend washed away.

After I'd been there a few minutes, Logan asked me, "How was your weekend?"

It was a glorious question, asked with sincerity and love. His desire was to reconnect with me, to hear about my experience, to get a sense of what had transpired in the three days since I'd last seen him.

And yet, there was indifference in the question too—in the best possible way.

He wasn't very much concerned about how this weekend went. It certainly wasn't a big deal. I could have said, "It was a disaster. They booed me off the stage!" and it wouldn't have interfered with the peace and love we were all experiencing around that fire pit.

My acceptance into this familial ring was not dependent on my performance in the classroom—or really anywhere. Here I am, Mom and Wife; my love, my humanity, my imperfection, my willingness to show up—these are the things that have earned me this space. Nothing about my outer achievement in the world.

On that day, I really got at a whole new level how much having this safe place to land supports me in taking risks.

No matter the complexity of the weekend—the highs and the lows—coming home to my family is a soft place to land. The place where people love me regardless of how well I performed or whether people liked me. They are a warm pool of acceptance for me to swim in.

On those weekends I realized it was SO much easier for me to risk, to be bold and courageous, to walk through the year, wig in place, eyelashes thinned, knowing these three people had my back. Knowing the whole thing could blow up—and they would still love me.

Carolyn:

Teaching alongside Michelle with the class not knowing she was walking through a breast cancer diagnosis was no small thing.

When Michelle told Ron and Mary that she didn't want the class to know, they supported her 100 percent. And Michelle was amazing. To say she taught the program at the top of her game is an understatement.

I used to joke (and still do sometimes, a little bit) that there are some people who might secretly wish it was me who became ill and died, and not Michelle. I am aware that this sounds HORRIBLE and macabre, and not at all spiritually evolved or sensitive in any way.

Let me explain. Every class weekend when we taught at USM, during bathroom or lunch breaks students could come and talk to the faculty: me, Steve or Michelle. When the breaks occurred, I started to notice students were lined up to talk to Michelle and Steve. I on the other hand, had a short line. Maybe one or two students. I didn't make a lot of this initially.

Eventually I started to joke about it with Steve and Michelle, "Look! I have all the time I need to go to the bathroom, to touch up my lipstick, check in with my family!"

Michelle and Steve usually did not. Michelle would often say to me as the seating music began to let people know the break was ending, "I need to go to the bathroom."

I would look at her and say, "Not me—I had PLENTY of time."

And we would both laugh and laugh.

Steve finally said to me, "I'm going to change seats with you in the back of the room. It's the location of our chairs in the back."

We did, and it was different. Not for Michelle, and just a little bit for Steve and I.

I still laugh about this. It makes me happy to know this happened. I really don't think it had anything to do with people liking me less than Michelle. I think it had more to do with who Michelle was and the quality of loving and support she exuded in the classroom.

Of course, people might have liked me less—it's certainly possible. I was known for being very direct, and that wasn't always easy for some people. Even though I was also known to be very funny, sometimes—for some people—the funny did not outweigh the difficulty of receiving uncomfortable coaching.

Nowadays I exude those qualities of loving and support and

humor and directness—for the both of us. I'm not kidding. I often feel like I *am* Michelle when I'm facilitating in front of a group, or meeting someone for the first time. There was a way Michelle had of connecting—her warmth, her interest, her caring—and it feels like I have absorbed it. I don't put up my shell of, "Please leave me alone for five minutes."

I don't have time for that anymore.

— 18

Arguments (or Lack Thereof)

by Carolyn

When Michelle and I were working together, people often asked: "Do you have disagreements? Do you have challenges working with each other?" Even though we seemed to get along so well, many people in our USM community figured there MUST be something we didn't see eye-to-eye on. How could there not be?

The basic answer is no, not really . . .

We had a few moments that were very minor in many ways. I'll share two that I remember, and how we approached them.

The first: We were running one of our coaching groups for women. Things were going well, and Michelle and I were handling e-mail—a lot of it. We had a clear communication with participants around email: we'd respond within twenty-four hours during the week, and possibly longer or not at all on weekends, unless it was urgent.

The problem in my eyes was that Michelle was responding much sooner—sometimes within an hour or less. She was up earlier than me, so she'd be on e-mail. I was awake later, but even when this wasn't an issue I'd sometimes wait to respond because I didn't want to give our participants the impression that we'd respond within fifteen minutes—at 11:00 at night, much less.

Michelle, however, wasn't waiting. And every day that she responded more quickly, I grew more and more frustrated. As I saw it, Michelle was now being the coach who responded more to our participants. She was looking like she was "on it" more than me—and I was definitely not okay with this. What's more, it was not the agreement! I felt like Michelle was wanting to get more connected to everyone, and as a consequence she'd get more individual clients from the group—and I'd be left in the dust.

I wasn't neutral. I was seeing her as against me. I wasn't happy. Nor was I in the most generous place in my thinking. At the same time, I didn't want to have to get on e-mail all the time so that we'd be "equal."

So what did we do? We had a session with our coach, Steve Chandler.

We got into it. Uncharacteristically, Michelle was not really seeing what I was seeing. In response to me expressing my concerns, she was saying things like, "I just want them to get a response . . . I just want us to be responsive . . . And I'm able to do it."

I said, "We had an agreement, though. And it's looking like you're more responsive, and like I'm not being there for them at the level you are . . ."

This went on for a bit, until finally Steve looked at her and said, "If your partner is feeling like the two of you aren't on the same page, and she's wanting you both to keep to your agreement, you might want to look at that."

Michelle stopped. She looked at Steve, then me, and it was clear a realization had opened up in her. She said, "I'm sorry. I wasn't seeing this. I'll stop doing the emails like that. I don't want you to feel that way."

And that was it. Michelle pivoted. It was over. She got it. I felt better, and she saw that we didn't want to train our participants to think they'd hear from us at a moment's notice, whatever time of day.

The other disagreement between us that comes to mind was after her second diagnosis. She was very sick. We were in the car because I was taking her home from a doctor appointment. She had her oxygen with her.

We were talking about an idea I'd had for holding an event on friendship. I'd been having a lot of feelings about our friendship, given her condition. And for the first time in our relationship I wasn't sharing them all with her—because, well, because she was dealing with a whole other thing: being sick, and undergoing all the treatment and emotional issues that came with it.

I was—in a passive way—trying to tell her that I was challenged in all of this. I shared that I thought it would be great material for a workshop. We could talk about friendship—what it means and what it requires. I said, "I bet a lot of women would come . . ."

We were driving; my eyes were on the road and not Michelle. She said, "I'm not really thinking about friendship. I'm dealing with a life-threatening disease. I'm dealing with trying stay alive for my kids, and doing everything that involves."

She did not say this gently.

And I did not receive it gently. I got very quiet.

We didn't talk more about it, but I understood.

I understood that I did not understand. What *I* was experiencing—the impact of the illness on our friendship—was something she simply did not have the bandwidth for. She was in a different place, a much more urgent one. For her, it wasn't about our friendship.

It was hard, and it made me aware that for perhaps the first time we were having *very* different experiences, and Michelle couldn't meet—much less help—me in the experience I was in. Nor could I truly meet her in hers. I did my best, and I still couldn't truly understand—not then.

Those are the two "big" disagreements we had. No knock-down dragout fights, no slamming doors, no festering emotional upsets that we carried around for months. I don't even know if they rate as much—but they were important.

We rarely had friction between us. I do remember Michelle saying to me once, "You care more about certain things, so I'm willing to do it your way."

Having said all this, I will add that I'm almost certain this dynamic would have changed if Michelle had lived longer. If she had, we likely would have had more disagreements. Why? Because we each would have changed, and there would have been points at which we would have had different thoughts about what we wanted in our professional and personal lives. For example, Michelle's sons are older than my daughter, so she would have been an empty-nester earlier than me, and maybe this would have inspired her to take things in a direction that I couldn't take myself at the time.

And of course, we—as are all of us—were experiencing ongoing changes internally, and who knows what would have unfolded as we explored life more deeply? Even after her initial breast cancer experience, Michelle was already thinking about things she wanted to do differently.

We had a very, very, very good working relationship, in large part because Michelle meant it when she said, "I'm more committed to your success than I am to my own." And because I was willing to serve Michelle until the very end, through the door of this life into another.

And we had a very, very, very good friendship. We laughed so much, texted so much, talked so much. We had something that is so rare, and it worked.

I am forever grateful for this. And now I coach business partners into greater generosity, greater willingness, and greater compassion and communication with each other. All the while creating more financial success.

— 19

The Worst Year

by Michelle

In January 2013, I was diagnosed with breast cancer.

It was just a few weeks after my forty-sixth birthday. In my mind, I was healthy, happy and busy. Really Busy. I didn't have cancer on the calendar for 2013. It was such a shock to receive the call informing me that, yes, in fact, I did have breast cancer.

I was no stranger to cancer. Both my mother and my mother-in-law had battled breast cancer almost fifteen earlier; my dear mother-in-law died at age 58 from the disease in 1999.

In 2012, my mom faced a diagnosis of tongue cancer and endured a ten-hour surgery in which part of her tongue was removed and then masterfully reconstructed, followed by radiation therapy boosted by chemotherapy.

Even though it was a shock to receive my diagnosis, cancer didn't feel foreign. I knew plenty of people who had walked this path before me and come out the other side just fine. I was determined to do my best to be one of those people.

Later that night, I called my parents to tell them the news. I had a heavy heart and sweaty palms—what must it be like to hear your child has cancer?

As I shared, my parent's response was surprisingly muted. My dad is a doctor and he asked a few questions. My mom was pretty quiet. I was grateful that they seemed calm and grounded. The message was, "You are going to be okay."

"Mom, I'm really going to need your support to get through this," I said.

There was a long pause on the other end of the phone.

"I'm going to do my best," my mom said. Another long pause, then: "Today I found out that my cancer is back."

Sock to the solar plexus. I didn't see that coming either.

Her tongue cancer had returned. Head and neck cancer is one of the nastiest around. She had already been through nine months of treatment, and now it seemed like her surgery and treatment from the previous year had done little to slow this aggressive cancer.

I realized that what I had interpreted as calm in my parents was more likely some combination of shock and numbness. Mine was only one more piece of bad news in what had already been a surreal day.

So began a year of surgery, chemotherapy, wigs, radiation, and doctor's appointments for us both.

It worked out that my mom's surgery was scheduled for two weeks after mine, with both of us having it done at the UCLA Medical Center. She was able to be there the day of my surgery and to watch my kids for the two days I was in the hospital.

It would be the last time she could step in and help me in such a full and active way. The last time she would have my kids sleep over at her house. My mom had been my nanny for seven years— from the time my oldest, Alex, was one year old, until my youngest, Logan, started kindergarten. At the time of my surgery, my kids were in eighth and sixth grade, solidly into adolescence. And my Mom continued to be a second mother for them. Her bond with each of my children was tight.

Twelve months later, in January 2014, I had a clean bill of health and an excellent prognosis. I had successfully navigated two surgeries, eight rounds of chemotherapy, the trauma of losing my hair and my eyelashes, and six weeks of radiation. I was grateful that every step of the way my doctors seemed relaxed about my prognosis, confident that I would be just fine. The year of treatment was difficult, but going through it while my Mom experienced even more intense treatment, with a bleaker prognosis, helped me keep my perspective.

My beautiful mom, luminous and radiant in her last days, passed away on January 12, 2014. She had endured her treatment with courage and grace. She had fought courageously and also found her way into acceptance. My mom had been my biggest supporter, my number-one fan, my back-up plan; she was there for me in large and small ways. We certainly had our mother-daughter struggles, but in all the years of being her daughter I never once doubted that I was loved—truly and completely loved—by her. So saying goodbye was the hardest thing I have ever had to do.

I would never want to sugarcoat the year of 2013.

From one perspective, it absolutely sucked. I cried a lot. I felt crappy and frustrated and sad. I hated losing my hair. It was hard to watch my mom endure her treatment. And coming into the awareness that she was dying was agonizing.

I wouldn't wish that year on anyone. I'm so glad it's over.

But as I was living through it—one trying day after another—I kept having the awareness over and over again: "This is NOT the worst year of my life."

"This is not the worst year of my life. This is NOT the worst year of my life. This is NOT the worst year of my life."

It was certainly the most intense year by far—but not the worst.

Given what was occurring, how could this NOT be the worst

year of my life?

Trust me—I was as stunned as you are.

The awareness that "This is not the worst year of my life" helped me see again how much I had grown in the previous decade. That year gave me an extraordinary and visceral way to appreciate the power of living a more conscious life dedicated to using love as a guiding principle.

Looking through the eyes of love, I was able to take in the immense blessings and learnings of this very challenging year:

This was the year my husband, Scott, looked me in straight in the eye and said I didn't need to earn a penny—my only job was to get well. And he proceeded to take over every household task I couldn't do, without hesitation or complaint.

This was the year my twelve-year-old held my face in his hands and said, "I love you bald, Mommy."

This was the year my fourteen-year-old willingly came to the grocery store, pushing the cart and unloading the car because I felt too weak to do it alone.

This was the year I called my mom just to hear her voice and ask her advice, knowing the privilege of talking to her daily was fleeting.

This was the year I witnessed my dad being a loving, steadfast partner to my mom, going to every doctor's appointment, sitting through every chemotherapy, dropping everything whenever he was needed. I watched him put aside his own fear to show up for my Mom, his partner for more than fifty years.

This was the year I got to see who my sister and my brother truly are—and watch them show up with courage and love for me and for our mother.

This was the year I got to thank my mom for all she's done for me, and help her appreciate the huge legacy of loving she leaves behind.

It was an extraordinary year, full of love, gratitude, support and connection. The year was full of what matters most to me: sharing loving and appreciating the gift of life. It was a year in which everything that matters most actually came *first*, and everything else seemed to melt away.

It was a hard year, but it was real and authentic and alive.

A hard year—but not the worst one.

The worst year, or YEARS in my case, were the ones when I felt stuck and trapped. The years I was afraid of pain, of failure, of setbacks, of discomfort, of embarrassment, of people not liking me, of people being angry with me, of people judging me.

These were the years when I believed my life was pretty much set in stone, that all the big decisions had been made—and that options for a different life were closed to me.

These were the years I believed that I lacked the courage, the skill, the talent, the energy, drive, luck, money, support to change my life.

These were the years that I judged myself as ungrateful, shallow, and a bad mom for wanting more in my life and for wanting to feel more engaged and alive.

These were the years that I would sometimes fly into an angry rage of frustration, screaming so loud my throat would hurt for days—scaring not only my children but also my husband.

When I was stuck in these "worst years," I would look with envy at people who seemed to be living more exciting lives. I really thought that they were "lucky" and that they were just built out of different stuff from me. That they had what it took to be courageous or to take risks. And that I didn't.

Through a series of miracles, coincidences and synchronicities, I found a way to transform myself and my life. I went from someone totally focused on avoiding pain and discomfort to someone willing to risk in order to do the things that matter most to me.

I am living proof that we don't have to be born with the skills or the willingness to live an authentic life—we can *learn* how to honor the unique calling of our own soul.

In many ways my journey began in earnest when I walked through the doors of the University of Santa Monica. Learning and living the practices and principles of Spiritual Psychology changed my life forever.

As I moved through USM's Master's Degree Program in Spiritual Psychology, which I started as I was approaching my fortieth birthday, I was astounded by how much I didn't know about how to effectively cultivate the kind of experience of life I wanted to be having. How much I had to learn about living a life of meaning and purpose.

Here I was, a lawyer, an executive at an entertainment company, a mother of two, a wife, a fairly educated person, and yet I was being confronted with how little I knew about taking full responsibility for having the life that I wanted. I was seeing how few skills I had at my disposal to work with my own emotional wounds and fears—and how lacking my traditional education had been when it came to that all-important skill of living a meaningful life.

Through my experience at USM, my life began to transform. First, my inner experience began to shift. I felt more hopeful, more peaceful, less afraid, less reactive. Then, over time, my outer experience changed too as I started to feel the inner prompting to share what I was learning with my larger community.

When I left my USM classes at the end of the weekend (once a month for two years) and returned to my life—my work in corporate America and my friends in suburban Los Angeles—all I saw were people who were just like me. Extraordinary, creative, talented people who also had a longing to share more of their potential in the world, who had secret dreams and a desire to do things that they didn't think were possible. Just like me, they sensed their own potential locked up inside of them, and they had no idea how to find the key.

But now I *did* know. At least, now I had some clues, some experiences, some skills that helped me and my classmates tap into more of our own truths and actually change our lives. I felt like an evangelist who had something essential to share with the world.

Eventually I understood that my deep desire to share what I'd learned, to share my own transformation, to teach the principles and practices of Spiritual Psychology, to learn as much as I could about supporting people in living their best lives in answer the call of their hearts—all of that was an expression of my own calling to coach others.

And with a mix of trepidation, excitement, hope, terror, and courage, I answered the call. I started on the path of being a professional coach, a decision which has brought a whole new level of joy and transformation into my life.

In the process of growing my business and growing myself as I coached, I've had the extraordinary privilege of working closely with my friend and mentor, Master Coach and the Godfather of Coaching, Steve Chandler. Being coached by Steve has taken my own learning to a whole other level. Make no mistake—I am a product of coaching. I would never have the business I have nor the life I have without the transformative power of that coaching relationship. The work we've done together over these last six years has deepened and expanded the transformation that started at USM.

Plus, I've been so blessed to have the spectacular Carolyn Freyer-Jones as a friend and a business partner. Carolyn was the light that led me to USM in the first place. Outside of my family, there is no one who has had as much influence in my life as CFJ. Working side by side with her has grown my capacity as a coach and as a person.

I have become a living, breathing example of transformation. I have handled so many fears, so many challenges, so many seemingly fixed outer obstacles . . . and I've come out the other side stronger, happier, clearer and more willing to keep going and keep evolving.

If I had any doubt about the power of the tools and skills I practice and teach, living through the year of 2013 dispelled those beliefs forever. I walked through that experience in ways that shocked me and humbled me. I was able to use my illness and my mom's passing for my growth, learning and upliftment (one of the cornerstones of a USM education). And I was able to face the challenges with courage, love and strength of heart.

When I work with my clients, they tell me how much they love the stories I share about my own journey of transformation. They love hearing how I've worked with my challenges and struggles. The bigger the screw up, the more value they seem to get from the story.

And in turn, I receive tremendous value from the love, strength and courage of my clients. The work we do together—the journey we take—becomes part of the body of experience and wisdom I'm able to share in the world.

If my 1998 self had read this story, if she had heard about the possibility of transcending fear and living more authentically, she would likely have said, "That all SOUNDS nice . . . but how do I DO it?"

Coaching (and writing this book) is my humble attempt to share what I've learned from living in that question.

Carolyn:

I'm currently in my "worst year."

We're in the middle of a pandemic, and my father died after being diagnosed with COVID-19, which he contracted in the hospital right before he was supposed to be discharged after receiving treatment for an unrelated health challenge.

My daughter had something occur to her that my husband and I learned about a week after my father passed, something that was very, very challenging to discover.

My husband hasn't worked in almost five months.

There's significant, important social unrest in the U.S., and I'm seeing how I have unconscious biases and hidden racism inside of me.

Did I mention we're in a pandemic?

The piece by Michelle that you're about to read took on new meaning for me as I reread it just now. I'll share more after you read it.

(Housekeeping note: If you've read this far in the book, you'll be familiar with some of what Michelle writes here, since she often used this as an introduction of sorts—a way to open people to a sense of what's possible. In this case, I don't think the repetition will do any harm, and in fact I hope it does some good.)

So: if Michelle only KNEW about 2020. Holy cow.

And yet . . .

Miracles are happening in the midst of this—for me personally, and for the world. My father's passing has been painful and deep . . . and I have seen my family come together and rise up in new ways that I didn't know were possible. My brother Paul has emerged as a connector, as a leader, which is both new and not new; he always showed inklings of these tendencies, but never quite embodied them until now. I'm discovering my own place as a way-shower for my nieces and nephews as to who we can be and what's possible during times of loss and challenge. My mom, always tough, is showing herself to be resilient and willing to evolve into a new life as she navigates the intense loss of my father, whom she was with since age sixteen.

My husband and I navigated the incident with our daughter with greater loving and neutrality than I could have ever imagined, all while I was wracked with grief. Together we are walking through the social unrest with a willingness to dissolve the hidden racism lurking inside of us, and we are committed to being part of changing the systemic racism that is embedded in the U.S.'s policies and systems. Inside of our home, there is still laughter, loving, joy and ease, even with my husband not working. Our daughter is experiencing us as not fearful of what's going on in the world (most of the time). She is hearing us talk about this being an important time to be alive, to be voices for loving, for humanity, and for true equality and freedom for all.

For the outer world it's a rougher time than any I have ever known . . . and yet the principles and practices of Spiritual Psychology are what I lean on inside of me.

"How I relate to the issue *is* the issue." "And "How I relate to myself as I go through anything" is the opportunity to "use everything for my learning, growth, and upliftment."

I'm grateful to have resolved enough of my own issues so that I lead a service-driven life, not an issue-driven one. There's never been a better time to be serving in the world.

— 20

What's the Message?

by Michelle

The last thing I expected in 2013 was a cancer diagnosis. I felt vibrant and healthy. I was fully engaged in my professional and personal life. I was deeply committed to my spiritual practice. In many ways, life had never been better. Never had I felt more on track or on purpose.

Learning that I had breast cancer felt like a swift slap to the mouth. I was stunned.

I'm grateful that I had the opportunity to work with one of my dearest teachers shortly after my diagnosis. I so deeply value her years of experience in working with people through difficult situations, her deep compassion and wisdom, and her commitment to growth. I was open to her thoughts about what I was experiencing and how to make my way through it with as much grace as possible.

In her words to me, there was no trace of "What did you do to bring this on yourself?" or "What did you do wrong?" Sometimes in spiritual circles the idea that "we create our own reality" can be used as a way to judge ourselves. There can be an assumption—spoken or unspoken—that if you have an illness, you've done something wrong.

Instead of judgment, she offered me an invitation: "Cancer is an opportunity for spiritual transformation." She reminded me of the possibility that this experience was "for me" and not against me, and that I had the opportunity to learn and grow in significant ways.

She offered me this perspective with such love and compassion that I was able to receive it as a gift. I avoided sinking into despair and blame, and I considered the possibility that I would grow from this in ways I would cherish. That I wasn't being punished—but rather groomed.

And she offered me another possibility. "Cancer," she said, "often comes with a message."

Just as these words were leaving her mouth, I knew what the message was for me: "Less MY will, and more THY will."

I had been saying for several years that my intention was to lead a Spirit-led life. Every day my prayer was, "God—given who I am, given my gifts, my skills, my responsibilities, my capacity—how would you use me? Show me how I can serve and who I am meant to serve.

I saw how in the previous five years I had pushed so hard to change my life. I had been so determined to change careers, so committed to getting all the learning I could out of my time at USM, and so consumed with what others were doing and whether I was falling behind or keeping up with them.

I was using my own will every step of the way.

— 21

Cancer Was Different than I Thought

by Michelle

My experience of completing each stage of my cancer treatment was different than I expected.

I expected to be elated when I finished my chemotherapy—and I *was* super happy. But the truth is I still had another round of chemo to live through—two more weeks of feeling like crap. And then after that came the slow realization that I was truly off that rollercoaster of rising and plummeting white-blood-cell counts.

Because I can get used to anything, I really did get accustomed to the two-week cycle of filling my body up with chemicals. First came the lethargy and nausea. Then, towards the end of the week, the crash of my depleted white blood cells, where nothing made me feel better. Not sleeping. Not reading or watching movies. Not eating sourdough toast slathered with butter (although I tried the sourdough toast approach over and over with the hopes of different results). All that was available was endurance. Eventually, as I got used to the cycle, I knew that in a few days the darkest period would pass and I would feel better.

One amazing thing: even at my weakest, even at my most

physically transformed (bald, no eyelashes or eyebrows, scars, tissue expanded in place of a breast) I still felt like myself. When I went inside—when I touched the core of my inner experience—there was no change. NO CHANGE.

I truly am not my body.

When I stepped into service to others, my physical limitations fell away. One night when I was feeling super weak and nauseous, I had a group coaching call to do—at 8:00 p.m. It was the one time during the whole four months of treatment when I felt like I might not be able to complete the call.

I prepared myself. I did my meditation. I asked for Spirit's Assistance. I made myself a delicious chocolatey, mocha drink (that for some reason seemed to help my nausea). And I prayed.

And you know what? A few minutes into the call, I was feeling better. A half hour into the call my symptoms had totally fallen away and I was engaged and present—inspiration was flowing through me and I felt great about the way I was able to coach our clients. When the call completed at 9:30 p.m., I was astounded.

Doing the work I do requires me to elevate in my consciousness. I have to focus on other people and not on myself. When I move higher inside myself, I feel better physically. This didn't always work (and I don't mean to suggest that when we are dealing with serious medical conditions or chronic pain that these aren't real phenomenon). But within the range of what we're dealing with physically, it's interesting to note how our perception of pain and discomfort changes based on what we're doing. How laughing impacts the way we feel.

If I hadn't experienced it myself, I wouldn't have believed it.

Prior to my cancer diagnosis, I had been asked to help develop and teach a new program at the University of Santa Monica, a six-month certificate program for graduates of the university's two-year master's program in Spiritual Psychology: Soul-Centered

Professional Coaching.

I learned about my diagnosis two months before the program was scheduled to launch, after it had already been announced to prospective students and we were well into developing it. And, of course, my diagnosis threw a big question mark into the mix. No one knew for sure whether I would participate fully, given my health challenge.

Yet this was such a special opportunity to work with so many of my favorite people: the teachers and mentors I love, my business partner and my coach. I didn't want to miss it. While I was absolutely committed to taking care of myself first, I set a very strong intention to participate fully. I scheduled my surgery as quickly as possible. and I partnered with my oncologist to develop my chemotherapy in a way that would support my teaching weekends. But, still, until I was in the middle of it, there was no way I was going to know what I could do.

The first big decision I had was whether or not to share my diagnosis and treatment with the class. I was teaching sixty-four of the most awesome, heart-centered people I knew. Many of them were former classmates and clients. All of them genuinely cared about me and for sure would have been supportive and loving.

It's a funny thing when you have a cancer diagnosis—even the best-intentioned people can say things that feel insensitive or unsupportive. Or perhaps what's more accurate is that people's well-meaning comments can poke at the places inside of you where there is fear. I experienced people wanting to be comforted by me and asking lots of questions: "How did you discover it?" "What stage are you?" "What kind of surgery?" And my least favorite question: "Did they catch it early?" And really they often wanted to comfort themselves, to reassure themselves that I was going to be okay and that they didn't need to worry about me.

Also, people love to tell stories about other people and their cancer struggles. Note to the world: any story that ends in a cancer patient dying from cancer is not a helpful story to tell the newly diagnosed. I know, I know—this seems like common sense. But you'd be surprised how often this happened. It's like people couldn't help themselves.

So I gave myself a gift: the gift of NOT sharing what was happening for me. Mostly this was a gift so that I wouldn't have to deal with other people's very well-meaning but ultimately unhelpful attempts to support me.

But this gift was also based on something else: my experience from job sharing back at Universal. For ten years I had worked three days a week—a reduced work schedule.

As a labor relations department, part of our function was to support all the motion picture and television projects currently in production (we could have fifty projects at different stages of production at any time). Each production had a labor executive like me assigned as the point person to be that production's main contact for any labor relations problem, question or challenge. This was a wonderful, fun and dynamic part of my job, and almost all of my contact with these productions was virtual. They were often producing these shows not just all over L.A., but all over the U.S. and the world as well, so we were very rarely in the same geographical location.

So my favorite game was "astound the client." I would start working with a new production, often with staff I had never met or worked with before. I wouldn't tell them that I "only" worked three days a week. I would just serve them. And, in fact, because I wasn't in the office every day (and therefore not dealing with long, drawn-out meetings and other commitments) I was often able to be wildly responsive—even on my days "off." This could be as simple as a quick email or a five-minute call. I never felt "resentful," because my days off were not meant for eating bon bons—I was still working, albeit as a mom, and it was generally easier to just get things handled immediately rather than waiting till my next workday.

And with the magic of technology (oh, how I loved my blackberry) I was able to stay pretty well in touch with work, even as I took my kids to school, orchestrated play dates and generally carried on the work of my days at home.

Then, after a few months of fantastic service, there was the big reveal:

"I only work three days a week."

My clients were routinely flabbergasted. They couldn't believe I could deliver such great service as a "part-time" employee. I loved it.

I imagine it would have been a very different experience with these clients if right off the bat I had said "So here's the deal: my work days are Monday, Wednesdays and Thursdays. If you reach out to me on Tuesday or Friday, I'll get back to you the next day. If it's really urgent you can send me an email." Blah, blah, blah . . . These were production people who routinely work fourteen-hour days. I can't imagine that that kind of upfront discussion would have engendered a feeling of confidence or support.

Much better to reveal after the fact.

I saw the same possibility with my cancer diagnosis and the Soul-Centered Professional Coaching Program. I had no idea how I would feel during my treatment—but I knew I didn't want scrutiny. The last thing I needed was sixty-four sets of eyes on me wondering how I was feeling, was I up to the task of teaching, did I look tired, or pale, or skinny, or sickly? I didn't want anyone paying too much attention to me. I wanted them to focus on the work.

And then, AFTER we were done with the class, AFTER I was complete with the treatment—of course I would share. I am a life coach after all: my job is to support and inspire. I wasn't going to hide this experience away, but I did get to give myself the gift of supporting myself through it in the way that felt best to me.

When I taught on the weekends, I would forget. Truly. I'd forget I was wearing a wig, forget that more chemo was waiting for me on Monday, forget, forget, forget—because what I was doing required me to be totally present with the students. In that space, I disappeared—in the best possible way.

In fact, as Sunday would continue and we'd head towards completion that night, the realization would begin to creep in. I'd remember that in less than twenty-four hours I'd be sitting in my recliner getting chemotherapy drugs pumped through the port in my arm and into my veins. I'd remember that I was about to start the rollercoaster of not feeling well again, of nausea, of fatigue . . . of nothing to do but endure. I remember one weekend—about halfway through my treatment— bursting into tears after class was over, just feeling so tired and not wanting to start the cycle again.

But during the weekends . . . it all disappeared.

During the weekends, it was all about being present.

During my whole treatment I only missed one scheduled workshop, which of course Carolyn handled with grace.

Recently, a woman I respect very much asked if I would coach her. She had been a student in the class. She said she wanted to work with me for two reasons. One, she appreciated how loving I was. She felt safe with me and knew she could trust me. Two, she was absolutely flabbergasted to learn that I was being treated for cancer while teaching that class. She said that if I could walk through that experience in that way, I was someone of true strength.

I was so flattered by this reflection. And grateful that what I had demonstrated was meaningful for her.

— 22

Losing My Hair

by Michelle

Isn't it crazy that the hardest thing about this cancer treatment was losing my hair?

The thing about losing my hair (at least for me), is that it was this side effect that really forced me to acknowledge what was happening. This side effect wouldn't let me pretend or ignore the fact that I was being treated for cancer. I was bald, for God's sake—this was happening; this was my life.

I don't even consider myself a particularly vain person. I've never been someone who saw my physical appearance as part of how I get power in the world.

A good friend of mine—a man who dated very beautiful women and married one of them—told me long ago, "You'll never meet anyone as insecure as a beautiful woman." His experience was that women who had been prized and appreciated for their beauty, and who used their beauty as currency in the world as a way to be "good enough," set themselves up for lots of struggle when their looks changed as they aged.

I smugly thought I had avoided that. I never rested my worth and value on my looks. I knew that my physical appearance wasn't solid ground for me. My being a "hottie" wasn't the basis of my marriage or any of my relationships.

(I had put my stake in the ground of achievement and success . . . Slightly different; no less painful.)

But dealing with being bald showed me otherwise. I am as vain as the next person. I care deeply about how I look. I've attempted to come to peace with all the ways in which my looks are lower than the general standard of beauty, but this was a new low, a new level of exposure.

These days, when I look at pictures of myself bald or with a little hair, I actually like them. I look at similar pictures of other people, and they look good too. But when I was going through it, not so much. It was hard for me to find my femininity.

My doctor gave me a very specific heads-up: I would start losing my hair between fourteen and sixteen days after my first chemo. She encouraged me to plan to shave my head to avoid the trauma of experiencing my hair falling out in stages. I scheduled a time with my hairdresser on day sixteen—making sure my girlfriends could be there to support me—and hoped for the best.

And, I'll admit, part of me hoped I'd be the one who didn't lose my hair. I'd be an exception, and for whatever reason my hair would hold on and stay in. *That* was a miracle I would have loved to experience. But sure enough on Day 14 I stepped into the shower and clumps of hair fell out in my hand. OH MY GOD—this was happening!

That was the first day of Spring Break, a day we had planned to spend with our friends at their beach house. I got out of the shower, dried my hair as carefully as I could and got ready for the day. After all, what else could I do?

It was a beautiful day at a beautiful house. My friend's kids are much younger than mine, so being with them helped bring out the playfulness and sweetness in my own kids. They had a blast playing in the sand while my friend and I relaxed and chatted.

We decided to walk to the pier for some fabulous fish tacos for lunch. It was a beautiful, long walk filled with exploration and climbing. And the tacos were really, really awesome.

By the time we were heading back to the house it was late afternoon. The wind had been steadily picking up, and now it was blowing fiercely, whipping through the coast and through my hair. And as it blew I could feel more and more of my hair falling out. It was wrapped around my neck and falling in my mouth.

I totally started freaking out.

Usually I would have hung out with my friend and her three-year-old boy, keeping her company as he picked his way along the shore.

But I looked at her and said, "I have to get back."

Alex and I started walking with purpose.

I had this image of being a dandelion, and this fear that a big gust of wind was going to come along and blow all my hair off my head in one fell swoop. I had an image of big chunks of hair blowing free and leaving unsightly bald spots behind. I also knew that this was highly unlikely since I had a very thick, full head of hair—but I nonetheless kept my head down and bolted for the house.

My nearly six-foot-tall son walked along with me. I was calm, but concerned. Finally I asked him, "Can you tell that my hair is falling out? Are there bald spots?"

"No," he assured me, "you can't tell at all."

And then he did something so unexpected and tender that I'll never forget it.

He gently and awkwardly put his arm around my shoulder.

No words, just a gesture of pure compassion extended to me, his mother, who was having a moment of absurd freak-out.

My eyes teared up as I felt his arm on my shoulder.

It was an astounding moment, and a beautiful few minutes as we walked together back to the house, his arm on my shoulder the whole way. Now both of us were in silence, me not worried so much about the hair. Me basking in gratitude for the beauty of this life, where we get to give and receive love at these tender junctions.

As I really took in the moment, I had the thought, "This moment makes the experience of losing my hair totally worth it."

The opportunity to receive such an authentic and tender expression of love from my son, a person whom I had spent the previous fourteen years nurturing. A chance to glimpse who my son really is, and the man he is becoming. To see his heart. To experience his ability to empathize with me.

And to feel once again how much more important love is than really anything else. Even hair.

— 23

Through the Eyes of Love

by Michelle

By outward appearance my client had it all together: three thriving teen-aged children, a loving husband, a beautiful home and an impressive career that had real meaning and heart for her. I knew her socially before we started working together, and I had always admired her strength and confidence.

After her father passed away, she reached out to me. She wanted help letting go of a feeling of insecurity and brokenness that had plagued her since she was a little girl. She joined a weekend workshop with Carolyn and me, and then after that our longer six-month coaching group. We supported her in releasing and healing misunderstandings about not being good enough.

She demonstrated tremendous courage and willingness as she let us see behind the mask of confidence that I'd experienced socially—and into the insecurities and fears that kept her up at night. She was a brilliant woman. She led a cutting-edge organization and she was practiced in using her intellect to navigate life. And she had used her analytical mind to dissect her own life in search of the cause of her current unhappiness.

Again and again her mind took her back to the story of how she and her husband had gotten engaged—a story that filled her with shame. They were living in Boston at the time and had been dating for three years. To her it seemed like "time" to take the next step and get married. In her late twenties, she had her eye on her biological clock and her life plan. And so she pressured a bit, prodded a little. Her then-boyfriend was unmoved; he didn't want to get married. He wasn't ready. They were at an impasse, and she felt hurt, rejected and confused. They stayed in this limbo place for several months, sometimes talking about it, sometimes not. She pulled away a bit from the relationship, spending more time with friends, licking her wounds, feeling sorry for herself that her boyfriend didn't want to marry her and embarrassed that she was the kind of woman who would have to beg her partner for a ring.

One day, she and her boyfriend spent the day together. For some reason, he went home that night, opting not to stay at her apartment. When he got home, he called and said, "Let's get married." She didn't know why (and still didn't when she worked with Carolyn and me). She didn't know what had changed.

But she also didn't ask. She just said, "Yes." And then they were engaged. There was no formal proposal. No down on one knee. No asking her father's permission. No thought-out romantic plan. The story she had told for more than twenty years was that he didn't really want to get married, that she had "coerced" him, that he felt like he had no choice, that she had decided on her own and it was the wrong decision, that their life would have been different if he had *wanted* to get married. She couldn't believe she was a woman who roped-in her man, and she still wondered if he regretted getting married.

"How long have you been telling yourself this story about your engagement and your marriage?" I asked her.

"Well, we've been married for more than twenty years . . . so at least that long," she replied.

"How often do you think about this? How often does this story run?"

She paused. "I think about it every day." This story had calcified in her mind and in her heart. It circled around and around, a continuous loop of regret that bled into her present-day life—holding her in a Svengali-like grip. She was unable to let it go, and this limited her ability to be present in the here and now and to let in the beauty of her current life.

Of course, I was thinking that after twenty years, if the man didn't want to be married to her he had had lots of time to get out. And, I'd seen him with her. It was obvious to anyone who spent any time with these two that this man adored his wife.

When I shared these observations with her, they didn't help at all. Her story rut was this loop about how he hadn't wanted to marry her. And it bred a well of insecurity, fear and regret. Had she married the wrong man? Should she have done something different way back then? Did he have regrets? Would she have been experiencing more joy, more connection, more love now if she hadn't pushed him?

Sometimes the job of a coach is just to break the pattern. Break the ironclad, calcified loop of thought that wears down a person like waves against a rock. If an interpretation of life events is causing repetitive distress, I know there is another way to look at what occurred that will produce a different emotional result. Sometimes I can be most effective just by shaking things up.

So with this woman, I issued her a challenge: tell the story differently. Pretend you didn't know your story. Pretend you hadn't been telling yourself THIS story every day for the past twenty-plus years. Pretend you were going to take a fresh cut at your engagement story. What if you were to look at your story through the eyes of love? What would you see?

"Treat it like a creative writing exercise," I told her. "I want you to literally sit down and write a new story. Don't change any of the facts—just look at it differently."

What she wrote was a love story. The story of a man who knew from the first few weeks of dating her that he wanted to make a life with her. After only a few months of dating, he went on a trip to Israel and he brought her back a gift—a set of Shabbat candle holders, telling her that they would use them in their home together. She remembered that when he left for the summer, he gave her his car to use, knowing she didn't have a car and that it would be a great help to her. She wrote about how trusting and generous this was, even though they had been together for less than a year. How thoughtful he had been to think of her in this way. She wrote about how his rock-solid support of her and what she wanted had never wavered—including moving across the country to support her career. She told the story of a man who had lived through his parent's volatile marriage and painful divorce—who was terrified of what marriage can do to people. A man who, especially while in his twenties, hadn't seen a close-up model of a happy long-term relationship. In fact, her own family had been a revelation to him— he had marveled at her parent's affectionate marriage.

As she told the story of their courtship and engagement through the eyes of love, she saw that he had always loved her, had always wanted to be with her. In fact, it was only his great love for her, his unwavering desire to make a life with her, that was enough to overcome his terror about marriage. His resistance to marriage had never had anything to do with her or how she felt about her. And his willingness to say "yes" to marriage wasn't coerced or forced by her. It was perhaps the truest and most romantic expression of love he could have offered. Way more vulnerable than a diamond ring in a glass of champagne at a fancy restaurant. Her husband saying, "Let's get married" was really him saying, "I love you enough to do the thing I am most afraid to do." He had said, "Let's get married" because he couldn't imagine not being with her.

Retelling this story from love changed her life. The old story about "something wrong" fell away; the fear that her husband resented her or didn't want to be with her dissolved. She saw her husband as courageous for saying "yes" to marriage, and for knowing his own heart—and not as a weak man who had been henpecked against his will into matrimony. And in the construct of this new story the love that had always been there was more visible and present in her life.

— 24

You are the Sun (a letter to a client)

by Michelle

My dear client:
    You are the sun. You are big and bright. You are wise and deep. You are the sun.

And sometimes the sun gets covered up by the clouds. If it's dark and stormy enough, it feels like the sun goes away. After all, the sky reveals no evidence that the sun was ever there. During a particularly brutal winter, people joke, "Will Spring ever come?"

But even in the darkest of times, no one doubts that the sun exists.

If the day is cloudy, that's not a problem. It doesn't change the nature of the sun. It doesn't impact the sun's brilliance or its warmth. It's just a cloudy day.

It can't be sunny all the time. Our eyes would burn out with the brilliance. We'd lose our appreciation for its sparkle. It's not supposed to be sunny all the time. Sure, different places (and people) have different climates. We can certainly move where the weather matches our preference. But even in sunny California there are weeks when it rains and rains and rains.

There can be great value in the darkness—great learning and nourishment. But it's much harder to see the value if we resist the cold and think it should be different.

So gather your cold weather gear and create your inclement weather action plan. What will you do when the freezing rain comes? The snow? The bitter, cold wind?

Will you panic?

Will you be like Chicken Little and declare that the sky is falling?

Will you be like the postal service? Come rain, sleet or hail, will you deliver what you are here to share, no matter what the elements present?

Will you put on a cozy sweater and curl up by the fire with a cup of tea and a good book or a good friend and know that it's only a matter of time until the sun shines again?

I am learning to be with my own internal weather. I lean towards sunny. I like to be up and happy and positive.

And I'm also grieving my Mom's passing. I'm learning to live in the world without her.

And when the rain starts to fall inside me, my initial instinct is to push it away. I don't want to feel sad. I don't want to be down. I don't want the pain.

But I am learning. Grief is my friend, not something to be feared. I will not be one of those plastic people who tape a smiley face over the depth of their sadness. I will not walk around pretending that my heart isn't broken.

I will not cling to grief either. I will not attempt to use it as a protection from being in the world, from being hurt again.

I will grieve well and fully. I will let the part of me that is bereft wail and cry.

I will sit in my chair, in my pajamas, under my soft blanket, space heater nearby, for days on end. I will float in the surreal experience of walking the Earth without my mother in the physical form, even as her spirit is so present with me always.

I will do all of this knowing that the sun is still there, burning bright, even if I can't see it, and I will know that there is nothing to fear inside of me. No place I can't go.

Because I am the sun.

Carolyn:

Michelle really WAS the sun for many people. Her family, her friends, her clients.

And Michelle was also showing us here that we are ALL the sun.

I love this:

"I am learning to be with my own internal weather."

Are you learning to be with your internal weather?

Since Michelle has passed I have fallen to my knees, bowing at the fountain of grief. Splashing my face with the water of my tears, initially bitter and angry at the people whom I perceived as insensitive, or bitter and angry at the people who didn't acknowledge my loss.

Splashing my face with my tears of loneliness, missing this person who knew me like no other, who loved me, who saw me in ways that no one else did, a true equal in thinking, seeing, feeling, working, expanding.

Splashing my face with my tears of wisdom, knowing that I am forever different now. Changed, deepened—I can and do hold the beauty and pain of life in my hands at the same time: laughter and tears, joy and sadness. The complexity of the human experience is clearer to me now, having walked through this.

Life's not boring. It's not for the faint of heart. My life is different now. Bigger. My life is bigger because I have more capacity to hold all of life's experiences—the "hard" ones and the beautiful ones.

I am grateful—I'm in a job where this deepening serves me well. I have a different understanding as my clients walk through their own life challenges. I have a perspective that all of this is GOOD, even if it doesn't quite feel good as we are walking through it.

— 25 ——————————————

Joy

by Michelle

A client said to me about her mom: "She got everything she's ever wanted, and she's never been more miserable."

Our wants can betray us. This is a great reminder for all of us to not be seduced by our wants. Sure—play, create, manifest . . . But don't be fooled by the idea that having what we think we want will bring us joy or peace or happiness.

All of us have equal access to joy. No one has more access than anyone else. Joy is not something that is determined by how much money you have, or how much health. How many people love you or what you had for lunch. Joy is a place inside. It's a place to come from. It's a place to tap into. A giant wellspring.

It's just a few weeks since I received the news of my recurrence. The world looks so different. It's amazing new information. A health diagnosis, an unexpected challenge, a death, a loss—all such events mark a specific point in time. Before and after. When the event is significant enough we never have to ask questions like, "Was that before or after my mom died?" We always know. It's as if the color of the page changes, marking a new chapter in life that's so different from the ones before it that we'll never be confused about when we turned that page.

And, so here I am attempting to digest this news: there is cancer in my body. The cough I've been fighting for a month isn't some winter cold, but irritation caused by cancer cells floating in my lungs. The pain in my hip that has stopped me from doing yoga isn't just age or some issue relating to my scoliosis; it's actually a tumor growing there—slow and small—but a tumor nonetheless.

I am with Alex and Logan—my sons, my loves, my lights, my reason for being and for living and for loving. Truly the most important people to me—if I didn't know that before this time I certainly know it now. Because in the moment of diagnosis they were the only people who mattered. Loving them and protecting them and doing right by them.

I used to joke that if I really knew what motherhood required, I never would have said "yes." If I really knew how hard it was, how much it would take out of me, how much it would demand my attention, my growing . . . How much time and money it would require. How much it would cut into my travel and my social life . . . I never would have agreed. If I had really known how painful it is to watch someone you love so much struggle and learn. If I really would have known how hard it was to play the role of someone's mother—a role that necessarily requires them to rebel against you and resist you and hate you and make fun of you and rely on you. If I really knew what it would be like to learn how to love them unconditionally even when they made big mistakes—embarrassing mistakes. If I knew the heartbreak of watching them get their hearts broken—would I have ever said yes to this journey?

But when I heard the news that I was having another cancer experience, the answer, maybe for the first time, was "yes"—yes, I would still do it. Even if I knew how hard it would be, the depth of the challenge. Because loving them makes it all worth it. Loving them makes life worth it. It's not even about them loving me—I know they love me, and that's precious and sweet. But it's about what they do to my heart.

I see how that joking about "I'm not sure I would do it if I really knew" is more about my own protection. Hiding from the rawness and the truth of what it is to love this fully and deeply.

So I'm sitting with my boys—and really they are young men at sixteen and thirteen-and-a-half—Alex towering over me at 6'3" and Logan definitely a few inches taller than me, but still close enough in height that we can hug without an awkward leaning down on his part. But when I look in their eyes I see all the ages they ever were. I see the little boys and the babies, I see the ten-year-old and the toddler. I see them. And I'm filled with joy and love. It just bubbles up. There is no stopping it. I'm still afraid of the cancer. I still don't know what's going to happen. I don't know how long I have left on the planet—but then, of course, none of us do.

And notwithstanding any of that, I'm feeling joy. Unmistakable, irrepressible joy. Look at these boys! Look at their beauty. Look at the light in their eyes. Look at their preciousness. Their wholeness. Just look at them.

We are sitting in a booth at Fish Dish, a local grilled-fish place, not fancy, in a strip mall not far from our house. Scott has stayed home to scrounge for dinner. I haven't been able to stomach much food in the week since I learned of the diagnosis, so I'm certainly not eating grilled fish. But the boys are hungry, and getting them to agree on a place for dinner requires something akin to mediation, so I'm happy they've agreed to this place and I'm happy I feel well enough to take them.

And then—all this joy happens. I don't think they even notice. I am sitting across from them, while they are next to each other, elbow to elbow, eating charred salmon. Logan is proud of his healthy choice of no fries. Nothing at all special or noteworthy about this exchange. Anyone watching us won't give it another thought.

But . . . the joy that is bubbling up inside of me . . . the joy of being alive. The joy of being with these two beautiful beings, of getting to love them and watch them and show up for them.

It just rips my heart right open.

— 26

Will My Life Still Be Good?

by Carolyn

I found a talk tonight that Michelle gave at the Claremont colleges, her alma matter. It's a really good talk (see Appendix 2). I am struck and moved by one of the stories she shares about two clients whom we coached together, two young women who started out in our coaching groups. They were (are) highly accomplished young women.

These two young women are my clients again, right now. Just recently I reached out to them, because I wanted them in my coaching school. I have had my eye on them in the years after Michelle and I coached them, and we have stayed in touch. They came to Michelle's service. I coached one of their brothers. And now, they are back in my midst, having enrolled in my coaching school. I can't tell you how much joy this brings to me—to get to coach them again, to hear them refer to their earlier time with us, to have them talk about something Michelle said to them that they still think about and use in their lives.

That's the most amazing thing about this profession: it has a tremendously long shelf-life. There's literally no expiration date on this work. We can say one thing to a client (something we may not even, at the time, think of as a particularly effective or profound thing) that they reflect on and use the rest of their life. And it's likely not even *what we said*, but where it's coming from when we say it. As Drs. Ron and Mary Hulnick point out, "There is no technique or tool that is more transformative than the power of love. Love is the transformative agent."

And what's also amazing about this profession is that as we grow in our own consciousness, we can serve people in new and different ways—even the same people we have already served.

Who I am now is different than who I was when I was coaching these women with Michelle. I am older, yes. I am also more accomplished, having taught at the University of Santa Monica. I have more experience serving coaches and understanding the different challenges and opportunities we face in this (fantastic) profession.

I am also different because I lost Michelle.

When Michelle was becoming more ill and her passing started to become a very real (and rapidly approaching) possibility, I saw very clearly that I might be facing life without her. I had alternating experiences of being very, very scared, and then bouncing back into the here and now, taking care of Michelle and assisting her in whatever was occurring, including walking her to the final door of this life.

"What will I do? How can I live without her? HOW will I survive this?" were a few of the thoughts that started to run through my brain.

These thoughts were not where I stayed, because the here and now of being with Michelle and assisting her in the final days was where I kept my focus.

I remember a lot about this time, and I will share one important conversation with you right now. I remember being on the phone with Dr. Mary Hulnick, my friend, my teacher and mentor. She and Ron made themselves available to me as needed while I walked through this.

I share this exchange because it was no small thing. Mary asked me how I was doing. And I broke up, and responded, "Mary will my life still be good if Michelle dies?"

She said, "Oh my gosh, Carolyn. Of course it will be good. It will absolutely be good. You have your beautiful family. And you have your work. And Carolyn, this is going to deepen you. This is going to deepen who you are. We don't know what this means for you, and it will deepen you in ways you can't see or know right at this moment."

Mary was right.

(Mary Hulnick is almost, if not always, 100 percent right when it comes to matters of life and loving and growth and transformation.)

It might be helpful if I share HOW Mary was right. First of all in my experience goodness is always available. So now, externally the goodness in my life looks like new, beautiful friends, people who have appeared and become new places to put my love and attention. This includes new colleagues whom I love and whom I likely never would have partnered with if Michelle hadn't died. These are people I work and connect with regularly, who add to my work and vice versa. My life is also good because I have a much stronger sense of myself professionally than I would have ever dreamed of. For one thing, in 2019 I started a coaching school. I now have a school for coaches. ON MY OWN. With my name on it and everything.

It's a small school—only fifty students, once a year, for six months. It's a school for professional coaches to learn how to flourish in this profession. They come to learn how to grow their business, one meaningful, important conversation at a time.

Much of this school was originally conceived by Michelle and I, though our last conversations about it took place when Michelle was healthy. At the time we were considering our next steps and were teaching for our second year at the University of Santa Monica.

That school was not something I ever imagined or ever thought I would consider.

It's bigger than that though. I am becoming masterful in my work, in my professional contributions, in ways that could only come with more learning and growth, more experience and more experimenting.

There's my beautiful family, my husband and my daughter—endless supplies of goodness.

More importantly though, the goodness in my life is from the deep well of infinite goodness inside of me that has always been there—before Michelle, and now after Michelle. Also now, after my dad has passed. The goodness inside of us is waiting to be accessed—because we are goodness personified. Below all the mud and dirt of judgements, old stories, limiting beliefs and illusions, below grief and hurt, is goodness. That goodness is not able to be deleted by any circumstance or situation. It can be temporarily hacked by judgement, or upset, or pain—and it's always there. So my life continues to be good as I continue to experience painful and difficult things, like my dad contracting COVID and passing. Like my mom having her own health challenges and passing about one year later. Like my husband losing significant work during the pandemic, and more. Goodness—seeing goodness and experiencing goodness—is available. Sometimes it takes me a little longer to see it; I need my coach or someone else to point that out to me, because I still have blind spots. I'm still learning and growing and I can always come back into the goodness of my heart, and into the loving and joy of life.

So can you.

— 27

Be a Rebel

by Michelle

My morning Spiritual Practice can look like a battle between good and evil.

Or maybe it's a comedy of errors.

Most mornings I wake up very early . . . like 5:30 or 6:00 a.m. I sneak downstairs, anxious for some quiet time before everyone gets up. Son #2 is also an early riser. I feel like we play a daily game of chicken—who can get up first to claim dominance over the downstairs. He rushes to the call of his favorite form of worship: video games. It took me years to realize that I could ask him to mute his game while I meditate, so low was my resolve that the mere distractions of video game music was enough to have me throw up my hands in frustration or muddle through half-heartedly.

So each morning the still and quiet of this pre-dawn time is precious, perishable and likely to expire at any moment.

Each morning I have big plans: meditate, pray, visualize, journal, practice self-forgiveness . . . Lots of opportunities to ensure I start the day connected with my Highest Self.

So what happens?

The pull of the world, the things to do, starts in right away, even as I walk down the stairs in the dark.

My first stop is always my email. The part of me that wonders, "What's going on?" is so strong. That part wonders if something exciting has happened while I've been sleeping. It looks to email to determine whether this will be a good day or a bad day.

And so the inner battle begins. Part of me is galloping ahead to the day and all that needs to be done. Because I work out of my home, I feel like a quick-change artist. First, we have a full family morning experience, with everyone eating, getting dressed and ready for their day of school or work. And behind them is me—cleaning, straightening, putting away all evidence that any of them live here—so that the minute they walk out the door, my space can be magically transformed into the tranquil retreat center and slice of Earth dedicated to profound and permanent transformation in my clients.

~

"Why do I have such a hard time meditating?"

My client asked me this question with such earnestness and despair. She looked up at me with her doe-like, trusting eyes, as if I would have the answer.

I thought to myself, "Why do my clients ask me the same questions I'm asking myself?"

My client was an accomplished woman who knew how to get things done. She was an award-winning creative professional who had brought million-dollar projects into the world with tremendous heart and effectiveness, all while raising two beautiful kids, maintaining a strong marriage and being a pillar of her community.

So why was ten minutes of daily silence kicking her butt?

The same way it was kicking my butt?

So when my client asked me "Why do I have such a hard time

meditating?" I was surprised when an answer came to me. Clearly it was an answer meant for me as well as for her.

"Meditation is an act of rebellion"

"What?" she said.

"Meditation is an act of rebellion."

"Rebellion from what?" I'd piqued her interest.

"Rebellion from the small self, from the ego—from that part that lives inside all of us that says we are not enough, that we aren't doing enough, that we could be more, do more, have more. The part that would have us believe that we are behind, and that the only way to catch up is to 'do' like crazy. The part that is profoundly uncomfortable when we sit and connect."

And as I think about this more now, I see that when I skip my spiritual practice *I forget who I am.*

I start to buy into the idea that I am my to-do list. That I am the one responsible for the miracles in my life. My ego gets puffy. I get competitive. I start looking out into the future. When I take the time to sit with myself, I have at least a chance of remembering to be present in the moment for the true miracles that are always unfolding if I open my eyes. I have a chance to keep myself in the moment, where I can hear the call of my heart and the whisper of my inspiration. I can remember that I am the dance, not the dancer. I can allow myself to be an expression of the divine instead of pretending to be a master of the universe.

Carolyn:

I remember when Michelle would talk about meditating to the women in our coaching groups: "When I go inside to meditate, I imagine myself with a black leather jacket, getting on my motorcycle, flipping up my collar—and giving a big 'FU' to the world."

It made me laugh.
It still does.

— 28

Endings and Beginnings

by Carolyn

I'm at the hotel where Scott, Michelle's husband, is getting married again. It's almost six years since Michelle's passing.

My mom passed away a little over a month ago, and I'm in new grief—the grief of losing my beloved mom, whom I have cared for and been connected to for what feels like eight million years. She passed away a year and two days after my father passed from COVID in 2020.

So, what with the pandemic and all, it's been an intense year and a half.

I had no idea it would be like this. I thought I'd lost enough people to at least know a little about what it would be like to lose my mom, but I didn't. Losing my mom is unlike the grief of losing my dad, and unlike the grief of losing Michelle.

I am seeing Michelle's writing about the loss of her mom in a brand new light:

My beautiful mom, luminous and radiant in her last days, passed away on January 12, 2014. She had endured her treatment with courage and grace. She had fought courageously and also found her way into acceptance. My mom had been my biggest supporter, my number-one fan, my back-up plan; she was there for me in large and small ways. We certainly had our mother-daughter struggles, but in all the years of being her daughter I never once doubted that I was loved—truly and completely loved—by her. So saying goodbye was the hardest thing I have ever had to do.

My mom was very different from Sheila, Michelle's mom. Trudy could be one of the most challenging, difficult people—and that's not an understatement. Her upbringing was complicated and hard. She came from almost nothing. Her father was a gambling addict. She was the oldest of eight, and grew up poor. She and her siblings were often without much food or necessities like shoes.

At a certain point after her father had left the home, her mother put all the children into foster care because she simply couldn't take care of them herself. My mom was fifteen at the time and was put in a home for girls. This was where she discovered how intelligent she was. This was also where she discovered a greater level of cleanliness in her environment, as well as new friendships.

When her mother could, she brought the other children back home, but she told my mom: "You're okay—you don't need to come home." I think, but I don't know for sure, that what my grandmother meant was that my mom was old enough to look after herself.

My mother had mixed feelings about this. The foster care environment she had found herself in was more supportive and encouraging of her academic abilities and strengths as a person. But it was hard not to feel she was being rejected by her mother.

She met my dad when she was sixteen—and after that it was Hugh and Trudy.

Of course, there's a lot more to share—and I'm going to stop for now. I've been talking and thinking about a book about my relationship with my mom for a very long time. I was clear that I wouldn't write it until she was gone, because while I knew the book would be a complete honoring of her and the magnificence of who she is, it would also be unvarnished—and *my* truth: the difficult, joyful truth of rage, of upset, of discovery . . . and of ultimately choosing to heal and let it all go.

And that is, ultimately, what we can do with everything. I will grieve the loss of my mother's presence on this earth and I will adjust to my earthly parents no longer being on the planet, just as I am still adjusting to the loss of Michelle. I remain Hugh and Trudy's daughter, and Michelle's friend and partner—amongst the many identities I have. I am also aware that I'm none of these identities; I am much more.

And I will step more into my own ability to be shelter and support for others: my daughter, my husband, my friends, younger people to whom I'm connected, my clients and more.

And I will celebrate Scott's marriage to a wonderful woman. I will celebrate that Michelle's sons are here, joining their dad as he enters this new life. I will celebrate with Michelle's sister Karen and brother, Jeff, along with many others who are here.

Scott found new love, we have much to celebrate.

I'm thrilled.

And I know Michelle is too.

— 29

I'm Secretly Lazy

by Carolyn

I am a longtime crossfitter—over ten years.

People hear this, and without seeing me they think, "Oh, wow, she must be a ROCK of muscle and leanness. She must be SO FIT!"

I'm not. I was not blessed with those genes. So despite ten-plus years of crossfit three days a week—plus other stuff—I look pretty . . . average. I look like I take solid care of my body, and that's about it. No sinewy biceps, no bulging quads, no extraordinary abs. I admit this is disappointing to me sometimes, as in, "WHY don't I have rock-hard muscles? For the love of GOD, I work so hard three days a week!!!"

As I age it becomes more of a thing. My body is changing, and to maintain my average, fit body it takes more effort. I'm currently in an internal war about adding another day of working out, so that I'm doing something (ideally hard) four days a week.

See, in some ways, I secretly hate moving. I'm a lazy crossfitter—I do things at my gym ONLY because I'm told to, and because I'm with other people I like. I find it's more fun to do really hard, really un-fun things with other people.

If Michelle were here and I texted her about this, here's what our exchange might look like:

Me: I'm thinking it's time to add a fourth day to my workout schedule. A big part of me doesn't want to, and another part of me is saying, "Do this," because it's time. Maintaining this moderate level of fitness requires more as we age. All the studies show it's better to have more days where you're moving. AND the other part of me really likes days where I can stay in my pajamas all day, working, and never leaving the house. Hence, an internal war is happening.

Michelle: An internal war?? That's not good—let's talk about this. And btw I can't believe you do three days of crossfit! I gag at this idea. You are such a rock star of consistency!!!

Me: I hear you and my arms and my stomach are changing—post-fifty-years old. AGH!

Michelle: Internal war doesn't seem like it would lead to a peaceful outcome, though . . . Is there a more loving way about this?

Me: I hear you. I don't know—and I hear you. I wish it were easier.

Michelle: Wish what were easier?

Me: DOING this. Aging. Everything.

Michelle: I hear you. What's the alternative though—death? I did that. Let me tell you that as glorious as it is—that is, coming back fully into the experience of who I am as a divine being—I want you to LIVE a long life and be fabulous. You have so much to live for! You have so many people to serve! I haven't even really told you how proud I am of you—you have a SCHOOL!!!!!

Me: I hear you. It's exciting, YES, and school, shmool . . . What about my flabby arms? I feel so superficial that this is my primary concern and I'm using up precious book space to talk about it with you.

Michelle: Human body, human concerns, my friend. I love you. I love your arms too—I think you look amazing, btw!! And you did such a good job last night at that talk!!

Me: I can't tell you how much I miss you. Every talk I give, every time I'm in front of people, I feel the part of myself that has BECOME you. I'm so much warmer like you—so much more loving from the stage, and after talking to people.

Michelle: You were always warm, OMG, Carolyn!!

Me: Not like you though—and now it's different.

Michelle: So what are we going to do about the internal war?

Me: Can't you fix it from wherever you are? I'd love that.

Michelle: LOL. It doesn't work like that—as you know!

Me: Yep. I guess I'm going to make a choice to do this with loving. Make love, not war. Make peace. Be gentle with myself.

Michelle: Every time someone is loving and gentle with themselves, the ripples are felt everywhere. If you could see it Carolyn—it's like waves of color, over everyone. It's the most extraordinarily beautiful thing, almost too intense to look at. It's felt by all those around, and it's felt by different beings. What Ron Hulnick says is true: "Every time one person heals one issue, the whole of humanity moves forward," and that it's also, "Every time one person is loving with themselves or others, it's felt by all of humanity, and loving is magnified. The choice to choose loving becomes easier and more available to all those in the vicinity."

Me: I love that.

Michelle: Yes, so it really does matter. Everything we learned at USM: "How we relate to the issue is the issue," and "How we relate to ourselves as we go through the issue" is all true. It all matters. It's what we look at every day; it's what we look at after.

Me: This book will be done soon.

Michelle: It's going to be amazing!! I can't believe it—you have taken it and made it into something.

Me: Well, all the pieces were there from you.

Michelle: It couldn't be done without you, though: your voice, your story.

Me: Our story?

Michelle: Our story, shared in your voice, with me. I'm so glad Carolyn. Not that it mattered—and I'm so glad. GLAD because you aren't stopping. GLAD because the world is better because you are in it. It's such a good thing. The world needs good things—and you are one of them. I'm so grateful to you. You helped me get here in ways you can't know right now.

Me: I still wish you were here, so we could age into our eighties together, human bodies and all.

Michelle: I know—and look at who's in your life!!! You will be surrounded by people—beautiful people, I'm so happy. Happy you have beautiful friends who see in you what I see, who love you and really see your magnificence. You have love in your life in so many ways. You filled that spot with even more loving. This is good. And I can't thank you enough for staying connected to Scott, and to my sister, Karen.

I promise you Carolyn, life will be good!! It has a lot in store for you: pain, joy, excitement, adventures, great loving and great learning. I don't know everything (I can't), and I can see all the LOVE. We are allowed to see that.

Me: You promise?

Michelle: HAHAHAHAHAHA LOL. I promise as much as "I" can promise anything (it's really different in that way)—and I can promise you that life continues. It's true—I'm exactly as I was when I left, only more so. Hopefully I will meet you when you come—I say hopefully because I can't see that either, and you know I'll be there first in line if I have anything to do with it!!!!

Me: Do you really think I can do all of this? My life, aging, John and I, Lucinda, everything?

Michelle: If I can walk through what I did—which I could in part do only because of the loving you marshalled and co-created, the service you did by me (and the quality of that loving was looked at by angels on high with the most profound joy)—if I can do what I did, Carolyn, you can do your life. There will be pain—you and I both know now that this is part of the human experience. And you will shine and rise up. You will be a beacon of light and you will be a joy—and you will have joy.

Me: I love you.

Michelle: I love you more now than ever before. I see how amazing you are Carolyn—AMAZING! You can't see what I see. It's AMAZING!!! Tell Steve and Mary and Ron I said "Hi" and let them know how much they helped me. Give Scott a hug for me, and tell Laura her daughter is STUNNING, and AMY OMG!! Look at her go! Lucinda—John—so much love!! And Amber—she's a shining star, I'm so glad you snatched her up for your school! Life is good Carolyn—never forget this. It's GOOD, and you being there is GOOD.

So I might be a lazy crossfitter.

However, I will not be lazy about loving.

Friendship transcends disappearance: an enduring friendship goes on after death, the exchange only transmuted by absence, the relationship advancing and maturing in a silent internal conversational way, even after one half of the bond has passed on.

David Whyte
"Friendship"

Appendix 1

Remembering Michelle

There are many people whom Michelle touched and made a difference with—friends, family, colleagues, and more.

The coach/client relationship is unique. To be coached by someone is to open up a conversation of possibility where the sole focus is on you—your growth, your opportunities, your challenges, everything. It's entering into a space where creation occurs. A more fulfilling life can be birthed, important relationships can deepen, a new way of being in leadership can be practiced and developed.

I asked a handful of Michelle's clients and a few who participated in our groups to share about their experience of Michelle—what it was like to be coached by her, the quality of her presence, and the impact that she had on them.

What you are about to read is unusual: personal experiences of being served by one coach, Michelle Bauman. That's what makes this profession extraordinary and important: every coach is different, and what occurs between a client and a coach is unique to that relationship, to that moment in time, based on what's occurring in the client's life and what they are wanting to create or shift.

The seven people who contributed are very different from each other (even though a large number of them are coaches). It speaks to Michelle's skills and ability to serve a wide range of people so deeply and so well.

These people are precious to me. They were so thrilled to contribute to the book, to share their private experiences and thoughts.

Enjoy this rare, behind the scenes look at the profound difference one coach can make.

Rachel Langer

Professional coach, MA

I felt truly honored when Carolyn asked if I wanted to include a few words of remembrance about Michelle in this book. There are so many memories to choose from.

I remember the first moment I met Michelle. Carolyn was running interference for her at a conference because she wasn't feeling well. I followed them out of the building at the end of a long day, eager to introduce myself, and as I was speaking with Carolyn in the parking lot, Michelle smiled at me from a distance as she waited for Carolyn to finish. Even in the dim evening light, I could feel her warmth in that smile.

I remember getting an email from her and noticing that her email address was "innerwow." My skepticism quickly dissipated after spending only a few minutes with her . . . and I remember looking back and laughing at how little I knew before I knew Michelle.

I remember our first official meeting together when I went to her house for a coaching session. Though I have no recollection of what we discussed, I remember the energy and feeling of inspiration, of possibility, of human connection I felt when I walked out the door and back into the new life I could now see for myself after our two hours together.

I remember her sharing a story in a small coaching group about her insecurity around how well things were going in her life. She had been talking to her own coach about it, and he said to her, "Michelle, how good can you stand it?" I remember being so struck by that story and that question. How unusual and astounding. And I remember a time many months later when we'd gotten my life turned around to a much better place and she said to me, "Rachel, how good can you stand it?" I never thought I'd be in a position for that question to be relevant to me. And with Michelle's support, it was.

I remember her laughing at me at a workshop I attended, led by her and Carolyn, when I didn't even know what the workshop was about. I just knew that anything Michelle and Carolyn were doing was something I wanted to join in on.

I remember the gift she gave me at my baby shower. A small book with a handwritten note taped to the back that read, "To Rachel, one of the few kids' books that actually had ME smiling." And she was right. That book saved me many a late night with my infant daughter . . . I got to imagine Michelle there laughing with me, and it helped me get through those long nights.

I remember learning of her recurring cancer and being scared to lose her, fully realizing she wasn't mine to lose. I was so far removed from so many people closer to her, and still I felt the impending loss with emptiness and fear.

I remember staying the night with her in the hospital, and her coaching me from her hospital bed. She was trying to communicate when she couldn't really speak and I pretended to understand what she was saying so she wouldn't feel bad, so she wouldn't over-exert herself. Silly me. She saw through that in an instant and, frustrated, gave me a stern look right over her breathing tube and insistently rang the nurses button to request supplies so we could communicate in writing. She wasn't letting me off the hook even in her last days. With that stern look that I can still see in my mind's eye, she encouraged me to be true, even though it was painful and uncomfortable, a lesson I will never forget and one I am still working towards.

I remember sitting with her on one of her last days after walking into the hospital that felt so depressing. And yet, sitting by her bedside, listening to machines beep and whir, there was a deep comfort in being near her, knowing she was still there.

But really what I remember most of all was the incredible *feeling* of Michelle. In writing this remembrance, I had the opportunity to look back at the emails I had received from Michelle over several years. I reread them all, close to a thousand emails. And what struck me again and again was the *feeling* that came through—a feeling of hope, of encouragement, of true unconditional support, of a person who saw the goodness and potential no matter the circumstance.

I also found these words she wrote in an email to a fellow coach in a group I participated in:

"I see an even stronger place for you to come from . . . it's the place when you stop buying into the belief that your clients (or your prospective clients—or yourself) need to change anything to experience what's possible. It's the opportunity to be in love with where they are right now—and really and truly be OK with where they are—have absolutely NO NEED for them to change—even if they are experiencing pain or suffering right now. It's to really look at the situation through soul-centered eyes, to really give this person the dignity of their own process. This is great practice for you in trusting other people's internal wisdom. And as you sink into this— as you truly have no urgency for their growth or what you think they should do—you will find you can serve with even greater strength of heart."

Strength of heart is what I remember about Michelle. A strength of heart that I could *feel*, that poured forth a love and humor and wisdom and warmth in life that was immense and special and, thankfully, contagious. I couldn't be around her and not feel it. I can't think of her now and not feel it. Of all the memories I have of Michelle, the thing I remember most is this feeling she left me with. A feeling of joy, of lightness, of possibility, of excitement, of peace. A feeling that I can call up when I think of her, when I think of life and how good I might be able to stand it, a feeling I want to give to those around me as freely and openly and naturally as Michelle did. And though I didn't know her as well as many others, I knew her well enough to know this was her true super power: her incredible humanity, the *feeling* of who she was. And I know I am so much the better for having felt its powerful glow.

Aila Hale Coats

Professional Coach, MA

About Michelle

In 2013 I had a baby girl, Rowan, pass away during childbirth. At the time I was already coaching but not doing it in a way that was truly fulfilling or financially supportive. Shortly after she passed I had a slew of coaches reach out to me to see if I'd like some support.

I did need support with my grieving process, and I received that primarily through participating in a six-day spiritual psychology practicum with my husband and through some follow-up sessions with a USM trainer/therapist.

I did say yes to a few conversations from coaches who reached out to me. And what was really on my mind that I wanted support with was building my coaching practice.

After Rowan passed away I had a new clarity on how important it was for me to do work that I truly loved in this life, and to have this life feel satisfying and meaningful. I was ready to step into my work in a much bigger way.

When I brought up with two different coaches that what I wanted to focus on was serving other people through my work as a coach, I received some pushback—in the form of encouragement to continue to work within my own consciousness on healing myself rather than serving others.

Although, I'm sure this had some merit, it was not in alignment with me.

At some point during that time, Michelle and I had a two-hour conversation. I shared with her my concerns around focusing too much on building my practice and not enough on healing myself, and that even though I felt ready, I wasn't sure.

This is where Michelle changed my life.

She looked me straight in the eyes and said, "You don't need any more healing in order to serve people. You can do it now."

These words were medicine for my soul.

They struck me in a very deep way. It wasn't just about Rowan and healing from that. The truth is, I knew that I wanted to become a professional coach about ten years prior to Rowan, *but I was so fixated on healing every aspect of my psychology in order to feel qualified to coach that I just wasn't ever going to get to it.*

And this experience with Rowan might have derailed me forever without Michelle's certainty in seeing the truth of me. It would have been such a good, compelling excuse to continue healing work on myself rather than serve others. Nobody would ever question me on it.

Except Michelle. In several email exchanges she redirected me from focusing on my own insecurities to serving the people in front of me.

And look, I really do understand needing to take time away from everything in order to focus on healing and rejuvenation—but, at least in my case, a week here or there would have been sufficient.

I can feel it in my bones that if it weren't for Michelle, I would've dedicated my entire life to focusing on my frailties and my opportunities for healing rather than living a life that feels truly uplifting and in service. In the seven years since that conversation with Michelle, her guidance has served me over and over again.

Whether I'm feeling deep grief or temporary insecurity, when I turn my attention from myself and onto my clients or the people in front of me to serve, I feel uplifted. I feel a healing taking place on a deeper level *while* I serve others.

One of the most powerful things I learned at the University of Santa Monica was the power of a service consciousness. That in calling myself forward into a higher state of consciousness, in service to others, I am ultimately served as well.

Had I chosen to, I may have found value in spending the last seven years in an ongoing daily deep dive into my grief. But the magic and beauty of my life as it is now, serving dozens of clients a month, connecting deeply with my husband and my two young boys, I have no doubt that Michelle's words of wisdom, woke something up within me that was far more valuable.

Michelle pointed me in the direction of my own health and well-being. I may still be a work in progress, but I can serve *now*, and so can you, and in doing so, we are all healed and uplifted.

Amber Krzys

Professional Life and Business Coach, MA

Working with Michelle Bauman is one of the greatest gifts of my life. Who I am today is markedly different because of my time with her. I often say she saw me and what I was capable of before I did. She believed in me, and because of this I was more open and willing to believe in myself.

When I met Michelle I was unhappily single, in a significant amount of credit card debt and hustling hard to grow my coaching practice online. I was highly attached to having success on my terms via a flagship online program that would make me hundreds of thousands of dollars. The issue was that each attempt I made to create that program led to further debt and despair.

Inwardly I was ripe with self-judgment and shame. I felt like a fraud and a failure. My ambition and need to be special kept me in fast action so that I wouldn't have to face what was going on inside of me.

Enter Michelle.

I didn't really know Michelle at that time. We were part of the same spiritual community and I knew she was a coach who was on my email list, but that was about it. So it felt good and a little strange when she invited me to talk. Fortunately for me, I said yes.

As I rang her doorbell, I remember feeling nervous and unsure of what to expect. Thankfully, Michelle's warmth, sweet smile and heart-centered leadership allowed me to relax. For the first time I let myself be fully seen and opened up about everything: my debt, my fears, my self-loathing. I cried and cried, and Michelle held such beautiful space for me.

She asked some gentle questions that opened me up to new possibilities. She helped me to see the narrative I was running and offered her own experience of laying down her need to be special. She also shared about a different model for growing my coaching practice—one that was more heart-centered and rewarding with less frantic hustle. She even expressed her thoughts about how the online world was superficial.

I'm not gonna lie: that made me mad. I wasn't ready to let go of the grip on my dream of online success.

I was grateful for my one session with Michelle and decided not to work with her further because "I couldn't afford it." I left feeling cleaner on the inside and clearer on the outside. I was certain great change was afoot.

It took me another year and a half of struggling before I made my way back to officially work with Michelle. Here's the thing though: during that year and a half Michelle continued to champion me from afar. She sent me two books, paid to participate in a 10-day program I led and emailed me messages like this from time to time:

Dearest Amber:

LOVED your "Life by Me" post! So authentic and touching. LOVE following all the adventure and serving in your life via Facebook—I admire you and your crisp, bright voice! Have you seen this great article about coaching from the *New Yorker*

Magazine? It's a great one to share with people who don't quite get coaching.

With Loving, Michelle

The two years I worked with Michelle created exponential growth in myself, my work and my life. In the first year with her I made multiple six figures, paid off my debt and moved in with my then boyfriend, now husband. I changed my business model and started using the "Prosperous Coach" approach. I quickly enjoyed the slowed-down pace and deep, heart-centered conversations. More importantly, I lived into my strength, confidence, compassion and loving.

Michelle helped me to embrace the parts of myself that I judged. She wasn't afraid to share her own vulnerable "mistakes" in service to helping me come to greater acceptance of my own. Below is an example. You'll see her loving response to an email where I was in deep comparison with another coach I knew:

Thanks for all of this! It's always so interesting as a coach watching what others do—and navigating this territory. I've learned a lot about it in my own process—and I'm happy to share. And you sound pretty neutral about this person, which I acknowledge and appreciate about you. It's also OK if some part of you isn't :-) - we can use it for your growth and learning. I once heard Caroline Myss say that what causes people unhappiness is chasing after a life that's not theirs. It was so powerful for me to hear that—and it got me so much more curious about what is MY life—MY path—who am I called to serve?—who are my people to coach? Who do I want to spend my life energy with? Who is asking me for my help? Etc. I'm so much happier and more fulfilled when I'm true to my own calling. And I've spent plenty of time looking at what others are doing (and I'm not saying you are doing this Amber—I'm just sharing what's present for me)—attempting to use what they are doing to inspire me rather than listening to myself. And, it's an interesting process to discern what is inspiring in others—what triggers my own ego desire to be "special"—and what my heart truly wants. I see these questions as a big part of my health journey right now. And what I'm being prepared for next.

So seeing things with others—whether it's this coach or anyone else—can be very helpful and important in attuning to our own path—and clearing the ego material that would have us question what we are doing. AND it is also helpful in encouraging us to stand forward in our own truth. At least that's what been true for me in my own process.

Sending you lots of love, Michelle

MY path—that is the real blessing Michelle gave me. In fact, it was only after her passing that I created Fierce Loving, Inc. I realized Michelle loved me fiercely. She knew when to push "get your big girl pants on and go do it," and when to gently offer compassion.

It is my true honor and privilege to be a part of her legacy and carry forward her great gifts in the world.

Carrie Johnson, J.D., M.A.

The And

Of all things, I think I remember her voice the best. The calm tone. The loving lilt. The measured cadence. The way she said "yeah" with two syllables when she was listening attentively, like YEAAAH-uhh, a compassionate, "I hear you" nod on the first beat down-swinging to a comforting, "I'm here with you" smile on the second. I never understood how she was able to funnel her innate enthusiasm and pulsing energy into that soothing, even voice. She was a wonder.

Michelle's magic wasn't only in the way she spoke, of course. It was also in what she said. I was blessed with the opportunity to listen to her and learn from her in a variety of contexts during the far-too-few years we spent together. I participated in the groups and workshops she led with Carolyn, and she supported me individually on some discrete projects as well. I count those experiences among the most rewarding and valuable of my life.

Michelle and I shared a conviction that the language we use matters, and we both felt a deep respect for the precision of words. In our work together, we were never "trying" to do something, because "trying" implies that we are failing until we succeed; rather, we were "working on" or "making progress on" or "getting better at" something. We constructed "projects" to focus on our present actions, rather than setting "goals" that require a focus on future results. We debated at length whether "mother" is something I am or something I do. She offered her perspective on the crucial difference between "but" and "and" in exploration and communication; using "but" to link two clauses diminishes the first, while using "and" honors it.

Michelle was a master at the "and" of it all. She would listen, clarify, confirm, validate, accept, empathize. She would acknowledge with an affirming "yeaaah-uhh." Then, her eyes would twinkle, she would tilt her head slightly to one side, she would softly say "And . . ."—and out of her mouth would fly such a zinger, such a brilliant and insightful and profound observation that fully respected my perspective and lovingly offered guidance and gently demanded accountability and masterfully opened a new lens through which to see the world, that I often had to pause to reorient myself. She was gracious and patient in those moments, allowing me to catch up at my own speed, always waiting for me when I got there.

Despite the brevity of our friendship, her wisdom—in HER words, in HER voice—remains ever-present in my life.

When I'm facing uncertainty and fixating on risk and drowning in worry and catastrophizing outcomes, I remember how she once simultaneously identified with and challenged the beliefs underlying these feelings. "Yeaaah-uhh," she said, nodding slowly in understanding. "I've lived through so many horrible days that never happened." I had never felt so seen. "And . . . how are those beliefs serving you?" Zinger.

When I'm struggling with the chaos of feeding and resting and shuttling and raising and loving the three young humans with whom I've been entrusted, I hear her: "Yeaaah-uhh. It's a lot. And . . . what if . . . what if this is the fun part?"

When I'm feeling betrayed or angry, when I believe that I've been wronged or misunderstood, when I'm indignant and entirely certain of my rightness and others' wrongness, I feel her gently tap my shoulder: "Yeaaah-uhh. I acknowledge all of those feelings. And . . . are you withholding love? Has any heart ever been healed by withholding love?"

When I'm experiencing disappointment or powerlessness or hurt, I replay one of our conversations. "Yeaaah-uhh. I can hear how frustrating it is that you aren't able to control this situation," she told me. "And . . . you get to decide whether you believe the Universe is ultimately a friendly place or an unfriendly place. And if you decide that the Universe is ultimately a friendly place, you can know that everything that happens—everything—is in service of you. That things happen for you, not to you. That whatever is unfolding is perfect, and is unfolding just as it is supposed to be unfolding for your growth, learning and upliftment."

She once asked me what I had learned in our work together that I never wanted to forget. I told her it was the questions:

How are my beliefs serving me?

What if this is the fun part?

Am I withholding love?

What if this is happening in service of me?

With these questions—with all of the questions she asked, the challenges she posed, the blind spots she highlighted, the dark corners she illuminated—Michelle taught me to have new conversations with myself, conversations that are both more gentle and more productive, conversations that begin from a place of possibility. For me, that is where Michelle lived. In possibility. And from possibility flows energy, enthusiasm, optimism, excitement, adventure, gratitude, creativity, confidence, action and, ultimately, love. These are Michelle's legacies in me.

I'm grateful for her voice in my head. I'm grateful for her goodness in my heart. I'm grateful for the myriad ways in which her loving has shaped who I am and what I say and how I do. I am better for having known her.

And . . . I wish I'd known her longer. And . . . I miss her.

Wendy Wright

Professional Coach, MS, MA, PCC

My first introduction to Michelle was in 2014 at a Women's Professional Development Workshop that she was leading along with Carolyn. At that time, I was working as a senior leader for a U.S. Government agency in Washington, DC, and I didn't know anything about coaching beyond the coaches I had on my sports teams.

When I initially decided to attend this workshop, I thought it would be an interesting event where I could pick up a strategy or two, meet some new people, and, with two young children at home, have a nice weekend away.

Well, I got that and a whole lot more! Though I had attended numerous professional workshops, this event was unlike any experience I had ever had. Typically, professional workshops present information and focus on skills and strategies that target an external change in behavior. Michelle and Carolyn introduced me to a completely different possibility. That is, they focused on creating an internal shift.

Up until this time in my life, I followed a very traditional path that I hadn't really questioned. I grew up in a family of high achievers; we were "doers"! Give us a project or a task and we will get it done. Life had always felt very busy and full running from one place to another and stacking up achievements.

Upon returning from that weekend, I started to slow down and began to get really curious and challenge my beliefs. Is it true that security and comfort are something that is "out there"? Does my happiness depend on someone else doing something? Can I heal my hurt feelings even if the other person doesn't acknowledge their role in my upset? Is it true that I am NOT my thoughts? Is money not equivalent to security? All of this was running through my mind when I sat down to write my "key learnings"—multiple pages, typed—and sent them to Michelle.

One of my earliest exchanges with Michelle was simple and yet so impactful. I shared a specific challenge and asked how I could handle a specific situation (really, my question was, what can I do?!). Michelle shared the following message with me:

> Wendy,
>
> No strategies are needed—often simple awareness is curative.
> And if there is a strategy, it's going to be how can you be more loving, gentle and supportive with yourself—not the harsh taskmaster—to fix this?
> Nothing needs to be fixed—nothing is wrong.
> All you are seeing is opportunity.
>
> Love, Michelle

What?? No strategy? Just building awareness? How is awareness "curative"? Don't I have to do something? And then introducing the concept of how I am being with myself. This was mind-blowing, and it kicked off a journey that opened up an entirely new world for me.

Michelle and I started to write back and forth. I started to see possibilities that I had never considered before. Michelle was incredibly loving, patient and curious. I began to see that for transformation to truly occur, it must take place inside of you.

When she finally proposed that we work together, I felt I had won the lottery. This was especially shocking to my husband when I told him that I was prepared to hire Michelle as my coach and pay a small fortune to do so. But he quickly was supportive when he saw how clear I was inside about making this investment. In addition, my family noticed that the way I was showing up had dramatically shifted. I was more patient and intentional, and—most importantly—I was "finding the joy." "Finding the joy" is something Michelle introduced to me early on and which has been a game-changer. That became my mantra when I would fall into the pattern of overwhelm because of everything I had to do. Michelle would ask me to "consider what if this is the best part of your day?" What a revelation!

I started to really slow down and get curious about what was truly in alignment for me. I started to realize that although the patterns I created may have served me at one time, they no longer did. And all the while Michelle was right there with me, shining the light on those parts that I had covered up with my busyness and focus on external (as opposed to internal) validation.

When an opportunity came up at work for me to participate in a one-year fellowship that focused on executive leadership, I took it. And it was during that year that Michelle and I formally entered into our partnership. As I became more intentional and built more awareness, I realized that coaching is something I feel passionately about and which aligns with my core value of connection. Now, seven years later, I am a full-time coach with a thriving practice, and I am living a life that fills me with purpose and joy.

The biggest gift that Michelle and Carolyn offered me in that very first workshop was that awareness and self-compassion are the key ingredients to unlocking limitless possibilities and creating the life I desired. While Michelle is no longer physically here, Carolyn and I have continued the work *along with* Michelle, who continues to fulfill the promise she made to me when we agreed to work together: "Wendy, I am 1000% committed to you and your process. We are partners." And for this partnership, I am so deeply grateful.

Shiva Fritsch

Chief People Officer, REGENXBIO

My Journey with Michelle

There is so much to say about the love and transformational experience Michelle created for me. She lives inside my head and my heart forever. I often hear her voice saying "Yes! Shiva, this is where you see with loving eyes!!" I know she is smiling upon me, upon all those she touched and was connected to.

Let me start from the beginning. I met Michelle in late 2013. I was a relatively content person with quite a lot of history "surviving" my life. I survived a revolution and a war as a little girl. I survived immigrating and assimilating into a whole new country and culture as an adolescent and young adult. Fast forward a couple of decades and I was just coming out of surviving an early breast cancer diagnosis and treatment when I met Michelle. We sat in a quiet and calming room in Santa Monica, California, one late afternoon and talked for more than two hours. She dove right into my heart and soul and pulled out my desire to want to THRIVE.

No more surviving! I wanted to THRIVE.

Soon after that first meeting with Michelle, I wrote her a big check and signed up to have her as my coach. My very first coach ever. We started our journey together in January of 2014. There is so much to share—literally over hundreds and hundreds of emails between us—and so many amazing life lessons. We laughed together, we cried together, she challenged me in loving ways, and she is always present with me. I hear her voice often. In her honor, I choose two memories to share that are clear anchors for my thriving journey.

The first was about having a growth mindset—learning that we have a choice every moment of every day as to how we relate to our life and our experiences. We cannot control anything that happens outside of us, yet we have the amazing ability to choose HOW we respond to our external experiences—and to choose to accept that what life brings us is for our growth and learning. Thriving requires a huge commitment and daily practice of choosing to accept this—regardless of what life brings our way.

Related to this, my very first exercise and "homework" with Michelle was that I had to send her one thing that I felt positive or loving about every single day—for ninety days! Well, at first, this was "fun." For about thirty days I sent her a daily email about what I felt happy, loving or positive about. I was proud of myself. Then . . . I started to doze off. I stopped sending the daily emails.

After a week or so, Michelle reached out and asked why she wasn't hearing from me on a daily basis anymore.

I wrote back simply, "I don't have much else to say daily."

She replied, "Shiva, let's get on the phone and talk."

In that conversation, Michelle used a lot of love to challenge me. She asked me how committed I was to growing and shifting my ways. She said "If you're not committed to a daily practice of some sort, then you're not really committed to this work together. I can send you your money back, and you don't need a coach."

WOW! What?? What was she talking about?

The fact is, she stopped me in my tracks and woke me up!

Yes, with that very simple statement: if you're fine and happy just the way you are, you don't need a coach. You only need a coach if you're committed to shifting your ways *now*, with daily practice. And there it was! About a month and half into our work together, Michelle made me look at myself and showed me the way. The way to creating experiences of love and joy, the way to thrive through growth and learning is to be committed to the process every single day.

The second life lesson I'd like to share from the many I learned from Michelle involves seeing and relating to others and the world from a loving place. Working with regular judgments and forgiveness. Michelle had me doing another daily exercise—this one only for a month—in which I had to work to be in touch with my heart and observe when and where I was not experiencing what was occurring around me with love.

She'd say to me, "No matter where you are and what you're doing pay attention to how you are seeing people. If you're at the grocery store buying your groceries, how are you seeing the checkout person? From a loving place? If not, what judgments might be present? How do you forgive those judgments and practice forgiveness?" In practicing this, I woke up again. I had been completely unaware of how little love I had on a regular basis regarding the world around me. I woke up to the many judgements that I held without forgiveness. I wasn't unkind—not by any means. I had just never really accessed the love within myself in the ways that Michelle was pointing me towards. So, I continued practicing seeing others and choosing to relate to them and my world with "loving eyes." That was our phrase, "Shiva, use your loving eyes."

Recently, with all that is occurring around us in the world, I pause often to honor the deep, transformational lessons Michelle taught me. Without these lessons, there might have been a lot of suffering and surviving occurring for me today. Instead I have learned with enormous love from Michelle that I have the choice to use everything that is occurring around me, and around the world, for my growth and learning. And what's more I can choose to *be* this way in the world, and to lead others in this way as well.

Until the very end of her life, even from her hospital bed, Michelle coached me. Even when I could hear how it was challenging for her to breathe, she wanted to keep talking. She'd say "Shiva, coaching is what brings me the most joy!"

Michelle Abend Bauman, you continue to shine brightly every day through all the lives you touched, transformed, and loved. I am eternally grateful for the gift of YOU!

Sandy Sullivan

Co-founder, the Alchemy Group
Professional Coach and Facilitator

We are both misfits.

The first time I met Michelle, she was a participant in a Leadership course that I led in late 2008. Her beaming smile, hand-on-heart reaction to various content, comments and palpable curiosity filled the room. At 7:00 the first evening, Michelle came up to me and declared, "We are both misfits." From her point of view, we both were working in a corporate setting with souls designed for upliftment. Michelle seemed to me to be like one of those sponges where if you add a drop of water they wildly expand. That is Michelle. Michelle asked me to coach her for three months, and in those three months she put the finishing touches on her wings to fly and departed her corporate job as an attorney and committed herself to a life of service as a coach.

Michelle called me in early 2010 and offered to coach me. "InnerWow" was her email. I thought, "Yes, she is energetic, intelligent, intuitive and I can help her by being one of her first clients." She shared the cost of her coaching and my InnerWow was more like a BOOM. Our first three calls were about, "I have two small children—I can't afford your fee." It became clear (and scary) to me that I was not going to help Michelle by being one of her first clients—she was going to help me. That was the beginning of a journey where one misfit guided the other misfit, and I know I received infinitely more value from Michelle than I paid for.

So much valuable coaching from Michelle, and the three learnings that stand out today, and which I pass along to many, are these:

1. Limitation creates value.
2. Listen to the inner self—she has something valuable to say.
3. Its okay to say "I am no longer okay that . . ." That's the beginning of a breakthrough

For me, Michelle's coaching is like fine wine: the value and taste (applicability) get better with time. When Michelle passed away I did three months of grief work with a shaman, and in that work Michelle was guiding me the whole way.

The shaman asked me, "Was Michelle world-class?"

"Yes."

"Are you world-class?"

"No."

Michelle's passing gave me the space and courage to finally shed the final remnants of misfit and step into the GOLD of what is possible in my life. I consciously don't miss Michelle—I see and experience her in so many places in my life and in my thinking. I am grateful to have been served by Michelle. Her service, for sure, changed my life.

Appendix 2 ———————————————

Claremont College Talk

Creating a Context for Success:
Leading Yourself so that You Can Lead Others

Presented by Michelle Bauman on February 7, 2014 at the Berger Institute, Claremont-McKenna College (Michelle's alma mater).

Thank you so much for having me here today—really it's such a thrill to be here at the Athenaeum—the site of so many happy memories for me. And it's such an honor to be address a room full of talented, accomplished, ambitious women of all ages. Really there is no group of women I'm more committed to serving than women interested in leadership and their own success. Today I hope to share with you some of the most transformational things I've learned about women and leadership.

I'm going to talk with you for a little while—and then there is going to be time for me to answer questions and really talk about whatever is most pressing for you as you contemplate your own leadership. I know it can take a lot of courage to ask a question in a group like this, so I actually have some gifts for anyone who asks a question . . . because I really want to be sure I help you and that I'm talking to whatever is most important to you. So as I talk, I want to invite you to pay attention to what questions you have or how you see what I'm saying can apply in your life (or not). That would be really fertile grounds for questions.

As you heard in that nice introduction, I have played and I continue to play many roles in my life. I'm an attorney by training and I practiced law for eighteen years, and for the past six or seven years now I've served clients as a coach. In some contexts the work is called "executive coaching" or "business coaching" or "life coaching"—but the bottom line is my work is about human potential. How do each of us be the most we can be, contribute to the world in a meaningful way, create lives that thrill us—that feel deeply satisfying and fulfilling? How do we maximize our potential? How do we have lives that resemble the truest version of ourselves? The self that we all sense is lurking inside somewhere?

Author Steven Pressfield observed that each one of us has two lives: the life we live, and the unlived life within.

I have the fantastic job of helping people live their unlived life.

As you heard, I have a law degree and a master's degree in spiritual psychology. I'm also a voracious reader and consumer of all things growth and development related, and I've just signed on to work with my own coach for a fifth consecutive year.

And even with all of that, all I'm really an expert in is my own life and what I've seen happen in the lives of the people—especially the women—that I serve. And today I am mostly going to be talking to you about the one choice—the one turning point that all my clients have gone through on their way to move into greater leadership, greater success and greater fulfillment. It really is the consistent turning point that seems to be required to step into more of our potential. The good news is that once you see it, it's learnable. It's available for us to practice—and it changes everything . . .

But before I tell you what that choice is . . . I want to tell you a little bit about my own life.

I wasn't always so enthused about growth and expansion.

I have a vivid memory of being nine years old and being on the playground of my elementary school—and realizing that this childhood thing wasn't going to last forever. That at some point the gig of being a kid was going to be up; I was going to be expected to go out in the world and provide for myself. And given that I came from a nice middle class family, I realized that in order to continue to live in the style to which I'd become accustomed, I had two choices, as far as I could see from my nine-year old self: I could fall in love and marry someone who could provide that life for me, or I could figure out a way to earn that money myself. And to me—at least at nine years old—finding a way to provide for myself financially seemed way easier than marrying into a life of security.

So on that afternoon, on the yard at Highland Oaks Elementary School, I made a decision. In order to protect myself, in order to find some security and safety in what seemed like a great big scary world, I would create financial security for myself.

And for about the next thirty years virtually every decision I made was vetted through this lens—my decision to go to law school was absolutely motivated by my absolute desire to create security for myself. In fact going to law school was the "easiest" way I could think of meeting my goal of being able to provide for myself financially, because no matter how challenging the academic experience was, when I graduated I'd be a lawyer.

This decision affected who I chose to marry, where I lived, what car I drove—even sometimes what I ordered for lunch. It was all about attempting to create safety and security for myself.

In fact, if you had met me circa 2006, what I would have told you about myself is that I am a risk averse lawyer. That I am SO risk averse—that my husband and I are BOTH risk averse lawyers, that we are financially conservative . . . That we are risk averse, risk averse, risk averse . . . I probably said this out loud at least once a day, and it probably ran inside me a lot more than that.

Now by the time it was 2006 I had in many ways created exactly what my nine-year-old self was wanting. I had a great job at NBC

Universal—I was the vice president of labor relations. I had a flexible work schedule so that I could work mostly when my two sons were in school. I had a great husband and a healthy 401K. I even had a minivan.

But you know what? I was profoundly unhappy. I was having the overwhelming experience of, "Is this all there is?" And feeling like everything exciting had already happened in my life. All the big decisions had been made, and now all that was left was to keep doing the same thing for the next forty years.

And, truthfully, that thought made me want to gouge my eyeballs out.

I was angry, I was resentful and I was bored. It wasn't pretty. And the people I loved the most—my kids and husband—were getting the worst of me.

Against this backdrop the University of Santa Monica and Spiritual Psychology entered my life. I dragged my husband to a weekend couples workshop at the University. It proved to be a turning point in my marriage—but even more so in my life. USM is highly transformational and experiential, and as I went through the weekend I had the experience of waking up—to my own dreams and potential—and I LOVED everything about it, to the point that participating in the two-year masters program suddenly seemed appealing.

On a break in the workshop I was walking to lunch with my husband and I was telling him how alive, engaged and stimulated I felt. I said I'd wanted to be a therapist when I was in high school and that I felt like I had missed my calling and wasn't sure I wanted to continue working in corporate America. I was literally talking a mile a minute—filled with enthusiasm!

And my husband, bless him, turned to me and said four of the most magical words I had ever heard:

"You should do it."

He floored me. That was the last thing I expected him to say.

My response was, "But honey, we are so risk averse. And this is such a risky thing to do. I don't know how I can move forward given that we are so risk averse."

And my husband looked at me with utter puzzlement and confusion, as if I had just spoken some foreign language. He said, "I'm not risk averse," and then proceeded to list all of the risky things he'd done in his life—all of which I knew. After all, I'd been married to the man for ten years!

And in that moment I saw clearly, perhaps for the first time. I saw that *I* was risk averse, that *I* had been holding myself back, keeping myself small. No one was doing it to me.

I saw that I had been afraid of life, that I saw life as something to be afraid of, to be protected from . . . and I didn't much like the results

And so began my journey of changing the way I relate to life. I enrolled in the two-year masters program at USM, where the curriculum is designed to help people answer the questions, "Who am I? What is my purpose? How can I make a meaningful contribution?" I couldn't believe I had lived almost forty years and still didn't know how to co-create, that these essential life skills about developing potential hadn't been shared with me. And when I went back into my life in corporate America, in suburban mommy-hood, all I saw were people just like me—people with their potential locked up inside of them.

And so began my new personal quest: to share my learning and my experience with as many people as possible, particularly women. And that's what I do now in my practice with individuals in the workshops and intensives I co-facilitate.

Context

Before we go any further, I want to offer a radical proposition. Are you ready? Here it is: context is EVERYTHING.

Context is EVERYTHING.

Everything we experience has meaning based on the context in which it's perceived. Context to us is like water to a goldfish—it's pervasive, it's essential, and it's so often missed.

Context is everything. It's how we create meaning in our lives. Context is the set of beliefs and understandings that we use to interpret what happens. Context is like a pair of glasses we're wearing all the time. It's the lens through which we see our lives and ourselves.

Context can be created consciously or by default.

You heard the story of how I allowed my nine-year-old self to create a context for a good chunk of my life. The context was: create financial security so you can be safe.

And each one of us has the power to reclaim the right to create our own context

Mindset

I want to offer to you today a powerful context, the one I've seen people use over and over again to become stronger leaders in their own life and for others.

To talk about this context I'm going to use a distinction that's perhaps best described in Carol Dweck's book *Mindset*.

(Which, incidentally, is one of the gifts available for those of you who are going to be asking questions.)

Prof. Dweck has spent her career studying the psychology of success, and what she's found is that when people have what she calls a "growth mindset," their ability to be successful grows exponentially.

In her work, she creates a distinction between a growth mindset and a fixed mindset. Let's talk a little bit more about these two mindsets and what they are. First let's talk about a fixed mindset.

People who have a fixed mindset start with a belief that our skills, intelligence, and ability to succeed are basically fixed.

Sure, maybe we can improve a little here and there, but our basic intelligence is what it is, and there's not much we can do about it. There is an underlying belief that certain people have certain gifts, that talent is what's most important in determining our success.

When we have a fixed mindset, we expect our experience in the world to show us where we rank, how successful we are, and how good we are. Everything that happens externally becomes either a reinforcement of our sense of self or attack on our sense of who we are. So if we think we are a good student and we get an A on an exam, we relax, we feel a sense of calm. Ahhh . . . We are good enough, we are as good as we thought we were. And if we get a bad grade on a test, we feel devastated. Our sense of self is threatened. *Oh my God, I thought I was good in this class, in this subject.* We feel vulnerable and exposed. We might even judge ourselves as not good enough.

Interestingly, Dweck's research shows that precious, intelligent children who received lots of positive reinforcement for being smart when they were young, are more likely to have a fixed mindset and have a much harder time taking risks and handling challenges. (That was me!!) More invested and attached to looking good and looking smart, and less likely to do things that might threaten their sense of self.

But people with a growth mindset have a totally different context in which they live. They believe that we each have unlimited potential to grow and learn. That we can get smarter. Better. More skilled. They don't see mistakes or failures as having anything to do with their essential selves. They don't see mistakes as having information about whether or not they are "good" or "good enough." Rather they see mistakes as opportunities to grow, to learn, to get better. In fact, if things aren't challenging, they get concerned because they know if they spend too much time in their comfort zone, they aren't growing.

And Dweck's research shows again and again that people with a growth mindset experience greater levels of success and demonstrate a greater willingness to take on challenges and to stay with things until they succeed.

They don't see setbacks and failures as having anything to do with their inherent worth in value, with their intelligence. They see them as opportunities to grow.

What I see in my own work confirms Dweck's research. And what I really see is that when we are willing to have a growth mindset, not only are we willing to take more risks, we are also willing to take risks in areas that are the most meaningful to us. The areas where we want to invest our time and energy into getting stronger and better.

When I have clients read Dweck's book they all have the same reaction. They see places in their lives where they are fixed in their thinking, others where they have a growth mindset. We all do both of these things in different areas and at different times.

And we all have the opportunity to more consciously create a context in which we welcome challenge as an opportunity to grow.

Because we still live in a culture that celebrates quick success, that buys into the idea of instant gratification, we put celebrities on pedestals. We love overnight sensations. The hard work of growth remains largely unseen in the public eye.

I want to share with you what this looks like in practice.

And because we are here at CMC, I want to tell you a story of one of my twenty-something clients. (And as an aside, when I tell stories, not only are they disguised enough to hide the identity of my clients, but I also have permission to share about them and their learnings.)

This story involves two young, highly accomplished women whom my partner and I have a coached for quite some time. They excelled in high school, they went to top colleges, and both are accomplished artists. When they were still in college, they decided they wanted to create a business to help other artists learn how to market themselves and create a career. They saw how artists were great at spending hours and hours working in their craft, but terrible at learning how to create careers for themselves. They launched this business with great fanfare and support, winning a small business award and grant.

We worked with Sarah & Shannon over the course of a few years. They participated in several women's coaching groups that we do, and also worked with us privately.

They had developed an online marketing course to support their clients, and although people who did the course loved it, Sarah and Shannon were disappointed with the level of enrollment. They were challenged in getting new people to sign up.

So we brought this challenge into our coaching. One of the women—Shannon—was primarily responsible for the course and the enrollment. We started asking her some questions: How much time are you spending talking to people about the course? What's getting in the way of sharing about how beneficial people find it? What's happening when you share with potential clients about the program?

And as we were asking these questions, I could see her starting to fold up like a pretzel: arms crossed, legs crossed, head down . . . and you could feel how profoundly uncomfortable this conversation was making her.

So I slowed down and asked what was going on for her. My job as a coach is to make sure that what I perceive is actually what's happening inside of my client.

Sure enough, she was uncomfortable, even terrified—not just of talking to people about the course, but of failing. She perceived her partner as more skilled at talking about their business and enrolling new clients. She perceived herself as more behind the scenes, more content-focused. She was absolutely terrified that she wasn't going to be able to fill these courses, that she didn't know how to do it, that the people she talked with were going to be annoyed or angry—and basically that the whole thing would be a disaster.

This was such a great moment in the coaching. Because all of us (including Shannon, because she hadn't really been aware of how much this fear was holding her back) were able to see she was living from a context of "don't fail," "don't look bad," "don't screw up." Her fear of failure was preventing her from taking the action she knew she needed to take to meet her goals. But until that moment the context in which she was operating went largely unnoticed.

Shannon was this highly accomplished young woman who had achieved so much in her life, who on the outside actually looked like a risk taker: she'd launched her own business and was deeply invested in her creative vision. She was an accomplished artist. If you'd asked her, she'd say she loved to take risks.

And yet we'd found this space in her where she was worried about looking good. In my experience we all have these—and the more success we have in the world, the more vested we tend to become in looking successful. We feel like we have more to lose. We feel like struggles or failures are less okay, and that somehow they will detract from who we are.

What we offered to Shannon in that session, what we reflected to her, is that she was so very new at knowing how to talk to people about the course. She had only been doing this kind of work for a few months, and this kind of talk is a skill that can take many years to master. Just like it took many years to master the many other skills she already possessed. Was she open to the possibility that knowing how to talk to prospective clients was a skill she could learn rather than a competency that her partner had and she lacked? Could it be possible for her to see that making mistakes and missteps could be part of the learning?

Immediately she started to loosen up, to see the truth in the opportunity to learn.

Then I asked her: "How much do you believe in the course? Do think it's valuable?"

She said yes. The value was very high. She had seen firsthand what a difference the course makes for people.

We asked her if it would make a difference in people's lives and careers.

She knew it would.

We asked if her getting people into this course so that they could be served was worth her learning how to move through her discomfort.

She said yes. Keeping her focus on the people she was dedicated to serving—and really, this was her leadership coming forward—gave her the "want to" to move through this discomfort of having enrollment conversations. The "how to" aspect of this involved her learning to sell the course—but the desire to serve— her "want to"—would propel her forward.

We had a created a new context for her. Before, her (largely unconscious) context was, "Don't look bad, don't take on this new uncomfortable role." Now her context was, "I'm committed to serving people with this great course. I'm willing to move through my discomfort so I can learn.

Next we challenged her to track her time spent in conversation and to commit to at least two hours a day talking to potential clients about the course, and to email us every day about having done this.

And you can all guess what happened. The course filled. But even more important, Shannon had fun. She saw that she actually had the capacity to do this work, and that she was better and stronger each day.

Growth Mindset as a Tool

When you start to see this distinction between a growth mindset and a fixed mindset, it becomes a tool for you to use. I'd like to offer it to you. You can use it for your transformation, and not just as interesting information to consider intellectually.

This is something you can start to apply to your life right now.

When you feel yourself folding up like a pretzel—either literally or figuratively—you can start to get curious: *Where do I have a fixed mindset? Where am I worried about losing face? Where am I concerned about not being good enough? What am I imagining failure or disappointment means about me, about my life? Where can I use challenges and obstacles to grow?* You can locate the areas where a fixed mindset is operating.

When you find them you can transform your mindset. You can reclaim your context. You can use a growth mindset.

I'm going to share with you a question that I use over and over again with my clients, one they say has radically changed the context of their lives, one that helps them move from a fixed mindset into a growth mindset in a flash.

You might want to write this one down.

What if the challenge or obstacle you were facing were happening FOR you, as a GIFT to you, ONLY for the purpose of serving you? What opportunity is it presenting?

Let me give you some examples of how this works.

I was working with a woman who was filled with rage and

resentment that her husband wouldn't share more of his money with her. It was a second marriage for both of them and they kept their money separate. She felt so hurt by this dynamic.

So I asked her the question, what if this were happening for you, as a gift to you, only for the purpose of serving your growth? What opportunity is this challenge presenting?

And she knew immediately. She had an opportunity to complete her graduate school program, which she had started but never completed. And as soon as it was completed she would make more money at work. She saw how completing her training would not only bring her more money but would also let her share her gifts in the world in a bigger way and take more responsibility for her life.

This awareness then gave an empowered shape and direction to our coaching work together.

This one question transformed a situation from being a source of anger and frustration into an opportunity to rise up and grow. She went from feeling like a victim to feeling empowered and motivated—a total-growth mindset.

Another client was a twenty-something who had just started her own business and almost immediately landed a multi-million dollar contract. She was celebrating big-time. She had made it. Her business would succeed . . . And then a few months into the project, the client pulled the plug on it and it went away. She was devastated.

So I asked her the question . . .

What if this happened for you, as a gift to you, only to serve you and your growth? What is your opportunity here?

And she saw a lot. She could demonstrate that she was in the business for the long run. She could learn not to put all her business-development eggs in one basket. She saw how she was willing to give away some protections in her agreement with her clients in the name of landing a big deal. She got to practice not taking it personally, and to see that the client's decision to end the project had nothing to do with her. This is just what happens sometimes when you play in the big time, and you need to be willing to have these things happen. She saw that she intended to run this business for decades, and in that context the downside from this experience is a blip—but the upside is huge!

Again . . . she saw the ways we could work together to make her a stronger business owner.

Think of a challenge or obstacle or problem you are currently facing—it doesn't matter how big or how small—and look for the opportunity to create a growth context for yourself . . .

Another client was the executive director of a non-profit and she was experiencing conflict with one of her board members, whom she perceived as demanding, condescending and difficult.

So I asked her the question: what if this were happening for you . . .

And she saw her opportunity to stand forward in her leadership, and to be able to do it neutrally without getting upset by his behavior, without taking his communication style personally.

Once again, the path for our work together was set.

One of my favorite examples of this came from a client who went on a trip to Tahiti with her husband. It was their first trip away together since their children had been born, and for the first three days it did nothing but rain. And she sat inside and stared out the window.

And then she remembered the question.

What if this were for me? What if the rain were a gift to me? What is my opportunity here?

And she saw it was an opportunity to slow way down, to really be with her husband. She swore to me that the question saved her vacation.

Antifragile

One author and thinker who talks about these ideas is Nasim Taleb. When he was an MBA student at Wharton, he realized that the English language doesn't have a word that means the opposite of fragile. In economics they sometimes use the concept of "robust" as the opposite of fragile, but robust really means something won't be damaged by stress or chaos. Saying robust is the opposite of fragile is like saying zero is the opposite of negative. So Taleb introduced the concept of "antifragile"—that there are systems that actual grow stronger based on stress.

We see this in sports and in physical exercise really naturally. We know that when we go to the gym and lift weights, it hurts. We might be sore when we are done, but we know we are getting stronger. Our physical body is antifragile to certain kinds of stress.

Taleb describes the distinction between fragile, robust and antifragile in a way that I think is particularly poetic.

A candle is fragile to the wind. . . . a gust of wind can easily blow out a candle.

A building is robust to the wind . . .the wind can blow and blow— the building won't move.

But a forest fire . . . a forest fire is antifragile to the wind. You take a small forest fire and you add wind and–wow–it can just explode into something much fiercer, stronger and more powerful than it was before.

We all tend to be fragile when we think we have more to lose than to gain from a particular risk or challenge.

We are antifragile when we perceive the upside—that what we have to gain is greater than what we have to lose.

So let's say you're a student considering going into graduate school and you're thinking about taking a very challenge course. You realize you might get a grade that will negatively impact your

GPA. Your decision whether to take the course will be affected by how you evaluate the risk and the upside of taking the course. If you think your GPA might go down and negatively impact your graduate school application, you might not take the course. Or if you think the course will make you smarter and stronger—and in the longer term more successful, regardless of how it impacts your GPA—you might go ahead and enroll in the class.

Our fragility towards life depends on how we evaluate risk, and on the context we create for the upside of possible risk. And what I've seen when opportunity presents itself—when challenge presents itself—is that if we look for the upside, we will find it.

I don't want you to think I'm being Pollyanna-ish and falsely cheerful about challenges, sadness and obstacles. I know that challenges can be really, really hard to deal with.

Just about a year ago I received a diagnosis of Breast Cancer. I've spent a good part of the last year dealing with surgery, chemotherapy, wigs, radiation and the like, and I'm happy to say that today I'm healthy and I have a great prognosis.

In the middle of all this I made a decision: I was going to use the experience of breast cancer to grow and to learn. I can't tell you how much it helped to live in the context of a growth mindset and to make a decision to be antifragile in the face of this diagnosis—to know that no matter what I was going to use this experience to grow.

It didn't mean it wasn't hard or scary or sad or painful. The growth mindset is not a way to bypass human experience. What it has done for me is help me create meaning and find a way to use my experience for myself and in service to others.

This year I learned how strong I am, how capable. I learned that I am more than just my body or my hair. I learned how to give myself permission to say "no" to what I don't want, to ask for help, to let people support me, and to value my health. And I also learned that I can serve other people even when I don't feel great.

And that's just the beginning. I'm still learning from the experience.

And so from that place, what I want to end my comments with is a reflection to each one of you. No matter what the risk, what the failure or disappointment, you always have more upside than downside. No matter what life gives you, you can always chose to be antifragile.

Each of you is without a doubt a forest fire. I don't care if you're a college freshman or a college president. I don't care if you're twenty or seventy years old. You are a forest fire. There is so much potential inside of you waiting to be cultivated! How can I say this with such certainty? Because I've sat with hundreds of people and I've never not seen it to be true. I've never met anyone—no matter how successful or unsuccessful—who didn't have more room inside to grow. YOU can chose to be antifragile. You can use the wind to expand and grow. You can let yourself light up and set the world on fire!

Recommended Reading

Bandison, Devon. *Fatherhood Is Leadership*. Maurice Bassett, 2017.

Chandler, Steve, and Rich Litvin. *The Prosperous Coach: Increase Income and Impact for You and Your Clients*. Maurice Bassett, 2013.

Chandler, Steve. *Creator*. Maurice Bassett, 2019.

Chandler, Steve. *Death Wish: The Path through Addiction to a Glorious Life*. Maurice Bassett, 2016.

Chandler, Steve. *How to Get Clients: New Pathways to Coaching Prosperity*. Maurice Bassett, 2021.

Chandler, Steve. *Ten Commitments to Your Success*. Robert D. Reed Publishers, 2010.

Hulnick, H. Ronald, and Mary R. Hulnick. *Loyalty to Your Soul: The Heart of Spiritual Psychology*. Hay House, Inc., 2013.

Hulnick, Mary R. *Remembering the Light within: A Course in Soul-Centered Living*. Hay House, Inc., 2017.

Kline, Nancy. *More Time to Think - the Power of Independent Thinking*. Cassell, 2015.

Kline, Nancy. *Promise That Changes Everything: I Won't Interrupt You*. Penguin Books, Limited, 2021.

Kline, Nancy. *Time to Think Listening to Ignite the Human Mind*. Cassell Illustrated, 2018.

McGhee, Stephen P. Get Real: A Vital Breakthrough on Your Life
and Leadership. CreateSpace Independent Publishing
Platform, 2014.

Ruiz, Miguel. *The Four Agreements: A Practical Guide to Personal Freedom*. San Rafael, CA: Amber-Allen Publishing, 2017.

The Arbinger Institute. *Leadership and Self-Deception*. Oakland, CA: Berrett-Koehler Publishers, 2018.

Whyte, David. *Consolations*. Canongate Books Ltd, 2019.

Acknowledgments

Michelle

Although Michelle never got far enough into creating this book to prepare an acknowledgements page, I'm sure that she would have wanted to thank and acknowledge her husband Scott, her boys Alex and Logan, her sister Karen and brother Jeff, her parents Sheila and Robert, Drs. Mary and Ron Hulnick, her coach Steve Chandler and me.

Carolyn

There are a number of people who continue to stand by me, cheering me on and loving me through all of life's beautiful opportunities and challenges.

- My beloved husband, John, you are a steadfast and true believer in me. My love, I thank you for your willingness to show up again and again as we navigate this life together, laughing, crying, serving each other and all those around us. You are a fantastic husband who gives, who cares, who loves me fully, who reminds me not to jump into negative future fantasy quite so fast or so often. Thank you for standing beside me in everything—I'm so grateful.

- Lucinda, I love you. Thank you for being a great love and joy in my life. May you know this kind of friendship in your life, and may you know in your heart how loved you are, beyond words, always and forever.

- Scott Bauman, you were an extraordinary husband to Michelle, and you became my friend in the process of Michelle's illness and passing. I can count on you to cheer for the work that Michelle and I started, and I am so grateful to you for allowing me to share Michelle's beautiful words with the world. Thank you for your friendship.

- Alex and Logan Bauman, your mom's love for you knows no bounds. You will see it here in this book and you will have it forever. It is such a privilege to be part of your mom's life and her love for you.

- Steve Chandler, my coach—you were the first. You were before Michelle, you saw me in ways I couldn't yet see myself, you were willing to speak the truth to me in anything, to dare to show me things I was not willing to see, to teach me things I didn't know I could do, and to continue to help me create myself over, and over again—into an author, a leader of a school, a strong professional, and so much more. I'll never forget the promise you made me when Michelle died—you have stood in that promise and you have delivered—and then some.

- Drs. Mary and Ron Hulnick, if it weren't for you and USM, poof! My life as I know it would not exist in this current form. The principles and practices of Spiritual Psychology have been a foundation and guiding force in my life now for over thirty years. This love story, this book would not have been possible without them. Michelle's transformation, and then the navigation of her cancer diagnosis was made not only better because of you both and her USM education, it was made miraculous. Miraculous because Michelle understood that the loving could flood every circumstance and situation, every hospital stay, every relationship and conversation—even the ones that were not spoken out loud. Thank you for everything, always.

- Johanna Jenkins, thank you for always being there when I am scared and I am losing my way—for your steady voice, reminding me that Spirit is and will show me.

- Amy Hruby, what would I do without you? You are the rock of Gibraltar. You show up in the most dire, inconvenient circumstances and you make them better with your presence, your loving, your extraordinary and ordinary service consciousness. There's nobody else I want to buy bagels with before someone dies. There's nobody else I want to do carpool for kids with, there's nobody else I want to discuss TV shows or spiritual reality with. You are a friend among friends, the most solid of souls. As you are aware, Michelle saw what was possible in your life before it was even on your radar, and it's such a joy to see it all happening! As Michelle would say, "Thank God for you." I do, every day.

- Liz Goldman and Laura Segal—you were each there at the most important times, for me, for my family, and for Michelle. I'm so grateful to call you my dear friends, now and always.

- Stephen McGhee, you were the person who facilitated next to me as Michelle was ill, and you showed me that I could facilitate with other people and it could be (really) good. I'll never forget your kindness and love at that time. I'm grateful for you.

- Devon Bandison, you came along at a time when I was still grieving Michelle. Your New York ways were a balm to my soul! Your ability to joke and play as well as go deep are a great joy to me—thank you for our rich friendship and the willingness to support each other in this great profession. I look forward to our work together, and to our friendship and the many laughs in the years to come.

- John-Roger and God, thank you.

- My beloved parents Hugh and Trudy Freyer—you made sure I had enough to eat, that I have a (decent—maybe even a great) sense of humor. You instilled persistence, loyalty and initiative in me and you believed in me—always and forever.

About the Authors

Carolyn Freyer-Jones, M.A., has been coaching women and men for over 18 years, assisting them in their growth as leaders. Her clients include corporate executives, business owners and business partners, creative executives and more. She has supported clients in becoming more effective at leading, communicating, growing their businesses, strengthening relationships, transforming careers, and experiencing greater success and fulfillment.

Carolyn is a long time champion of women. She has developed and facilitated a series of dynamic women's coaching groups—"Self-Mastery for Professional Women"—as well as weekend intensives.

She was on the faculty of the University of Santa Monica (USM), where she developed the Soul-Centered Professional Coaching Program with Drs. Ron and Mary Hulnick, Steve Chandler, Michelle Bauman, and Stephen McGhee. She graduated with a Master's Degree in Spiritual Psychology in 1998 from USM and considers the principles and practices of Spiritual Psychology to be the foundation and springboard for her work in the world as well as her personal life.

Carolyn has her own school for professional coaches—the CFJ Coaching Success School—and teaches coaches the skills and tools for growing a financially thriving business that makes a difference in the lives of others.

She lives in Los Angeles with her beloved husband John and her daughter Lucinda, where she works out regularly (because she wants to—not just because it's good for her), serves her clients, and writes about coaching and life. She loves enjoying coffee (every single day) and traveling to faraway places.

~

Michelle Abend Bauman, J.D., M.A., was a coach, workshop facilitator, and speaker who supported her clients in living with greater strength, creativity and joy. Michelle started coaching in 2007 and developed a particular love of coaching small business owners, professional service providers and coaches. About half of her practice was devoted to helping these types of clients create more successful businesses and live more fulfilled lives—and often significantly increase their income in the process. With her friend and business partner, Carolyn Freyer-Jones, Michelle facilitated a series of coaching groups: "Self-Mastery for Women: Co-Creating an Inspiring Life," "Self-Mastery for The Professional Woman" and "Whole Life Transformation." These combined live workshops with group coaching to create transformative results. The hallmark of Carolyn and Michelle's work together was supporting clients in learning to release judgment, relate to themselves in more loving and supportive ways, and attune to and use their inner wisdom for guidance and direction. Participants in their groups, for example, launched new businesses, published books, returned to dating, and created more loving family relationships.

Prior to launching her full-time coaching practice in May 2010,

Michelle practiced law for eighteen years. After working as a labor and employment attorney in private practice from 1997 to 2010, she worked at NBC/Universal, most recently as Vice President, Labor Counsel. She earned her law degree from the University of Southern California, serving as an Articles Editor of the Law Review. She was a 2008 graduate of the University of Santa Monica with a Masters Degree in Spiritual Psychology and she completed the Consciousness, Health and Healing program in 2012. She was married to her husband, Scott, for seventeen years and their two sons, Alex and Logan were her greatest teachers and her greatest joy.

Work with Carolyn

If you would like to learn more about working with Carolyn or attending her school, or to have her speak at your event or work with your organization, please visit:

www.carolynfreyerjones.com

THE CFJ COACHING SUCCESS SCHOOL

This six-month school for professional coaches takes place annually from January through June. Coaches from the United States and around the globe participate, including students from Hong Kong, Germany, the UK, Greece and more.

The CFJ Coaching Success School is the only school dedicated solely to assisting coaches in learning how to build a financially successful business through slowed down, meaningful conversations. You can learn more here:

carolynfreyerjones.com/coaching-success-school

Made in the USA
Las Vegas, NV
10 April 2024

88510995R00142